MY NOTES ON ......

KINEMATICS

DINESH KUMAR JINDAL

This book is dedicated to all my students who always were keen to ask more and more challenging questions and, in the process, taught me to solve many a difficult problem via various methods other than my own.

Contents

CONTENTS

PREFACE

This book is meant as a complete theoretical material on Kinematics for entrance examinations like IIT-JEE (mains and advanced, both), NEET, AIIMS, BITSAT etc. It covers all the concepts of kinematics that are required to solve the questions that have been asked in these examinations for over last 40 years. It contains ample theory and in text exercises that make the readers able to solve any question thrown at them in these exams. The matter consists of what I have been teaching to my students to get them through entrance exams. I have tried to inculcate 25 years of my experience in coaching field in this series of books (more on the way). Besides entrance exams this book also serves the purpose of introducing kinematics to a newbie. Anyone with the knowledge of basic vector mathematics and calculus can easily go through the book and learn kinematics. Even if the purpose is just to gain knowledge, this book is one of the best tested ways to go.

Dinesh Kumar Jindal

29 June 2019

ACKNOWLEDGMENTS

The work on this book started when my students asked me that my hand written notes be published as a book. I'd like to thank my students to encourage me to compile my lectures into the book, My Notes on Physics. Dr. Richard Feynman has been a huge source of inspiration and been my idol since my college life. Even the title of my book owes a lot to his book's 'My Lecture Notes on Physics'. My sincere thanks to my student and son Mehul Jindal who converted my hand written notes into this book. All the illustrations and scientific typing work has been accomplished by him. Every aspect of book design is credited to him.

INTRODUCTION

Mechanics is one of the oldest discipline of physics. Comprehension of this discipline begins as one delves in the study of Kinematics. The arbitrary motion of objects around us has been the cause of our fascination since our childhood. The discipline of physics which answers all the queries about changes in the state of motion is called mechanics. Kinematics is that part of mechanics which deals with such changes without going into details of the forces which cause these changes.

In this book we're limiting ourselves to kinematics. Kinematical parameters that we're concerned with throughout the book are distance, displacement, speed, velocity and acceleration.

Rest and motion

I.   Rest and motion are relative terms.

II.   There is no meaning of rest or motion without the viewer (or observer).

III.   Nothing is in absolute rest or absolute motion. The object is said to be at rest when its position doesn't change with the passage of time with respect to the observer. If the object changes its position with the passage of time with respect to the observer, it is said to be in motion.

IV.   To locate the object, we need a frame of reference.

V.   Three mutually perpendicular lines intersecting at a point is called a frame of reference. The intersection point is called the origin and the three lines are named X, Y and Z axes.

VI.   When an observer is at rest with respect to a frame of reference, then the observer is said to be in that frame of reference.

VII.   The coordinates (x, y, z) of a particle specify the position of the particle in the frame of reference.

VIII.   If all the three coordinates x, y and z of the particle remain unchanged as the time passes, the particle is said to be at rest with respect to the frame of reference otherwise it is said to be in motion.

Concept of point mass

I.   When the size of the object is much smaller than the distance it moves in a reasonable amount of time, we can replace it by a point object or a particle to describe its translatory motion.

II.   A particle is the physical analogue of a point.

III.   When every part of an object undergoes displacement and each part has the same velocity and acceleration, we can describe its motion by the motion of any point of it. Such a motion is called pure translatory motion.

Types of motion

One Dimensional Motion

I.   It is motion in a straight line

II.   If we take any one of the coordinate axes along the straight line of motion, we can describe the motion by specifying only that coordinate of position which changes with the passage of time.

III.   Examples:
      a.   Free falling object under gravity.
      b.   Motion of a train on a straight railway track.
      c.   A man walking on a long, level and narrow lane, etc.

Two-Dimensional Motion

I.   It is motion in a plane.

II.   If we take any two of the coordinate axes in the plane of motion, we can describe the motion by specifying only two coordinates of position that change with the passage of time.

III.   Examples:
      a.   A billiard ball moving on the billiard table.
      b.   A lizard moving on a wall.
      c.   Earth revolving around the sun.

Three-Dimensional Motion

I.   It is motion in all round space

II.   We can describe the motion by specifying all the three coordinates of position that change with the passage of time.

III.   Examples:
      a.   A flying bird
      b.   A flying kite
      c.   Random motion of gas molecules.

Position of a particle

The position of a particle means its location in space as seen by an observer in a given reference frame. It is best given by the vector drawn from the origin to the given point, as shown in the following figure, the position vector of the point P is

$$\vec{r} = x\hat{i} + y\hat{j} + z\hat{k}$$

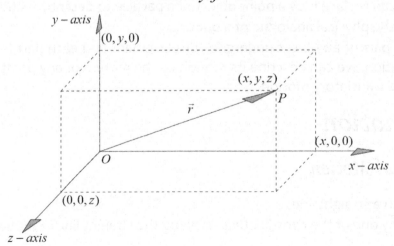

If the particle moves along a straight line then we can consider that line as x-axis and the position is given by the x coordinate only.

Displacement

The change in position of a moving object in a given time is called its displacement. It is a vector quantity joining from initial position to the final position of the particle. If a particle goes from A (x_1, y_1, z_1) to B(x_2, y_2, z_2) in given time, then it is clear from the figure that the displacements of the particle is $\overrightarrow{\Delta r} = \overrightarrow{r_2} - \overrightarrow{r_1}$, where $\overrightarrow{r_1}$ and $\overrightarrow{r_2}$ are the position vectors of points A and B.

$$\overrightarrow{r_1} = x_1\hat{i} + y_1\hat{j} + z_1\hat{k}$$

$$\overrightarrow{r_2} = x_2\hat{i} + y_2\hat{j} + z_2\hat{k}$$

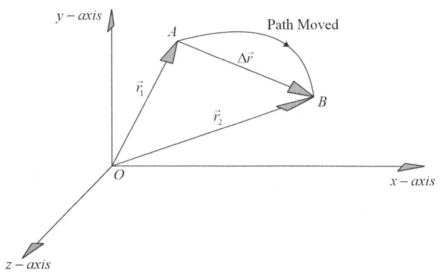

$\therefore$
$$\overrightarrow{\Delta r_2} = (x_2 - x_1)\hat{i} + (y_2 - y_1)\hat{j} + (z_2 - z_1)\hat{k}$$

or
$$\overrightarrow{\Delta r} = \Delta x\hat{i} + \Delta y\hat{j} + \Delta z\hat{k}$$

Where $\Delta x = x_2 - x_1$, $\Delta y = y_2 - y_1$ and $\Delta z = z_2 - z_1$ are x, y and z components of the displacement. Displacement can decrease or even it can become zero when the object returns back to its initial position. Displacement can be negative (as it is vector quantity).

Distance

It is defined as the total length of the actual path taken by the body between its initial and final position. It is a scalar quantity. Once a body starts moving, the distance always increases with time (or becomes constant when body stops), it can never become zero.

$$\text{Distance} \geq \left|\text{Displacement}\right|$$

Distance can be equal to the magnitude of displacement only if the direction of motion does not change. Distance can never be negative.

CAUTION

The quantities, Δr, $|\Delta \vec{r}|$ and the distance travelled, S, are entirely different. It must be carefully noted that $|\Delta \vec{r}| \neq \Delta r \neq S$. From the figure it is clear that $|\Delta \vec{r}| = |\vec{r}_2 - \vec{r}_1|$ is the magnitude of displacement which is equal to the length of the straight line AB. The quantity Δr is the increase in the size of position (or radial position) vector $\vec{r}_1$ which is equal to the length CB $= r_2 - r_1$. Clearly $r_2 - r_1 \neq |\vec{r}_2 - \vec{r}_1|$. The two quantities $r_2 - r_1$ and $|\vec{r}_2 - \vec{r}_1|$ will be equal if the particle moves along the straight line OC. Here, S is the length of actual path.

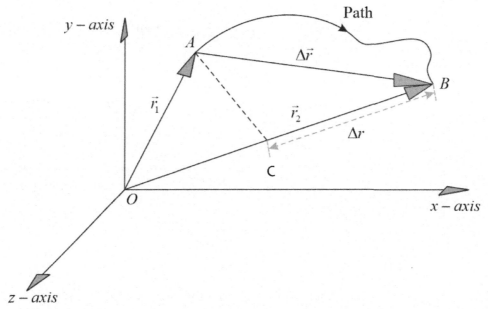

These three will be equal only if direction of motion does not change. When the motion is straight line motion along x-axis then, Displacement $= |\Delta \vec{r}| = \Delta r = \Delta x = x_2 - x_1$. In that case also the distance S will be equal to the displacement only if the direction of motion does not change

Average Speed and Average Velocity

Average Speed

$$\text{Average speed} = \frac{\text{Total Distance}}{\text{Time taken}}$$

It is defined as the total distance covered by an object in a given time divided by that time. It is a scalar quantity. Average speed can never be negative, and for a moving body, moving in any way, average speed in always more than zero.

Average Velocity

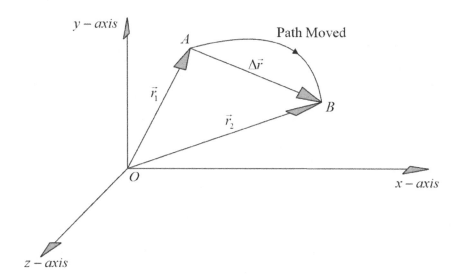

It is defined as the displacement in a given time divided by that time. It is a vector quantity; its direction is that of the displacement. As distance $\geq$ displacement. Average velocity $\leq$ Average speed. Average velocity can be zero as well as negative. When a moving body returns to its initial position, the Average velocity becomes zero.

$$\text{Average Velocity} = \frac{Displacement}{Time\ taken}$$

By definition, Average Velocity between points A and B is equal to

$$\overrightarrow{v_{av}} = \frac{\overrightarrow{\Delta r}}{\Delta t} = \frac{\Delta x}{\Delta t}\hat{i} + \frac{\Delta y}{\Delta t}\hat{j} + \frac{\Delta z}{\Delta t}\hat{k}$$

$\dfrac{\Delta x}{\Delta t} = \left(v_{av}\right)_x$ is the x - component of Average velocity.

$\dfrac{\Delta y}{\Delta t} = \left(v_{av}\right)_y$ is the y - component of Average velocity.

$\dfrac{\Delta z}{\Delta t} = \left(v_{av}\right)_z$ is the z - component of Average velocity.

$$v_{av} = |\vec{v}_{av}| = \sqrt{\left(\frac{\Delta x}{\Delta t}\right)^2 + \left(\frac{\Delta y}{\Delta t}\right)^2 + \left(\frac{\Delta z}{\Delta t}\right)^2}$$

CAUTION

The quantities $\dfrac{\Delta r}{\Delta t}$, $\left|\dfrac{\Delta \vec{r}}{\Delta t}\right|$ and the average speed are entirely different quantities, that is,

$\left|\dfrac{\Delta \vec{r}}{\Delta t}\right| \neq \dfrac{\Delta r}{\Delta t} \neq \dfrac{S}{\Delta t}$. For example, in circular motion, the rate of change of radius is zero therefore

$\frac{\Delta r}{\Delta t} = 0$, but neither average speed $\frac{S}{\Delta t}$ is zero nor the average velocity, for many of the time intervals, is zero.

Instantaneous velocity and Instantaneous speed

Suppose a particle undergoes a displacement $\overrightarrow{\Delta r}$ from time t to $t + \Delta t$. Its average velocity during this time is given by $\overrightarrow{v_{av}} = \frac{\overrightarrow{\Delta r}}{\Delta t}$, this average velocity will become the instantaneous velocity at time t when the time interval Δt becomes infinitely small i.e., $\Delta t \to 0$.

Thus, instantaneous velocity at time t is

$$\vec{v} = \lim_{\Delta t \to 0} \left(\overrightarrow{v_{av}} \right) = \lim_{\Delta t \to 0} \left(\frac{\overrightarrow{\Delta r}}{\Delta t} \right) \qquad \text{but} \qquad \lim_{\Delta t \to 0} \left(\frac{\overrightarrow{\Delta r}}{\Delta t} \right) = \frac{\overrightarrow{dr}}{dt}$$

(differentiation of position vector with respect to time).

$$\text{Instantaneous velocity, } \vec{v} = \frac{\overrightarrow{dr}}{dt}$$

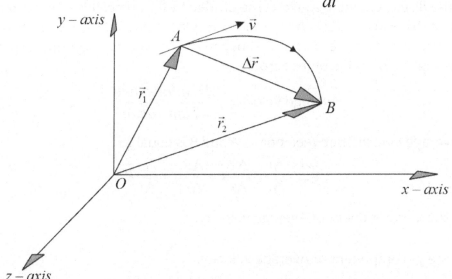

In an infinitely small time dt the displacement $\overrightarrow{dr}$ becomes tangential to the path, so the instantaneous velocity vector is everywhere tangential to the path.

writing $\qquad \vec{r} = x\hat{i} + y\hat{j} + z\hat{k} \qquad$ and $\qquad \frac{\overrightarrow{dr}}{dt} = \frac{dx}{dt}\hat{i} + \frac{dy}{dt}\hat{j} + \frac{dz}{dt}\hat{k}$

or $\qquad\qquad\qquad\qquad \vec{v} = v_x\hat{i} + v_y\hat{j} + v_z\hat{k}$

where $\qquad\qquad\qquad v_x = \frac{dx}{dt} \; ; \; v_y = \frac{dy}{dt} \; ; \; v_z = \frac{dz}{dt}$

As the distance travelled in an infinitely small time (ds) cannot be different from the magnitude of displacement $|d\vec{r}|$ in that time, therefore, instantaneous speed is equal to the magnitude of instantaneous velocity, thus,

$$\text{Instantaneous speed } v = |\vec{v}| = \left|\frac{d\vec{r}}{dt}\right| = \sqrt{\left(\frac{dx}{dt}\right)^2 + \left(\frac{dy}{dt}\right)^2 + \left(\frac{dz}{dt}\right)^2}$$

CAUTION

Only in straight line motion $v = |\vec{v}| = \left|\frac{d\vec{r}}{dt}\right| = \frac{dr}{dt} = \frac{dx}{dt}$. It must carefully be noted that $\left|\frac{d\vec{r}}{dt}\right|$ & $\frac{dr}{dt}$ are entirely different quantities. There are many situations like that of uniform circular motion in which $\frac{dr}{dt} = 0$ but $\left|\frac{d\vec{r}}{dt}\right| = v$ is a finite quantity equal to magnitude of instantaneous speed.

Calculation of Distance Travelled by a Particle in a Given Time

The distance ds travelled by the particle in time dt is equal to $|d\vec{r}|$ which is given by

$ds = |d\vec{r}| = v\,dt$. Therefore, total distance travelled in a time t is obtained as $S = \int\limits_{\text{for time t}} ds = \int\limits_0^t v\,dt$

and if v remains constant then $S = v\int\limits_0^t dt = vt$

Exercise 1

A particle is moving in x-y plane, with its x and y co-ordinates varying with time as: $x = A\sin\omega t$ and $y = A[1 - \cos\omega t]$. Find the instantaneous velocity, speed and distance travelled by the particle in time t. A and ω are constant.

Solution

If $\vec{v}$ is the velocity of the particle at any instant, then $\vec{v} = v_x\hat{i} + v_y\hat{j}$

Here, $v_x = \dfrac{dx}{dt}$ (x-component of velocity)

and $v_y = \dfrac{dy}{dt}$ (y-component of velocity)

Differentiating $x = A\sin\omega t$ with respect to time gives $v_x = \dfrac{dx}{dt} = A\omega.\cos\omega t$. Similarly,

differentiating $y = A[1 - \cos\omega t]$ with respect to time gives $v_y = \dfrac{dy}{dt} = A\omega.\sin\omega t$.

Therefore $\vec{v} = \dfrac{dx}{dt}\hat{i} + \dfrac{dy}{dt}\hat{j} = A\omega[(\cos\omega t)\hat{i} + (\sin\omega t)\hat{j}]$

and speed $v = \sqrt{v_x^2 + v_y^2} = \sqrt{(A\omega\cos\omega t)^2 + (A\omega\sin\omega t)^2}$

$\therefore$ $v = A\omega = \text{constant}$

7

Speed is constant $\therefore$ distance travelled = speed × time = $A\omega t$

Exercise 2

A particle is executing circular motion with a constant speed so that time period of revolution is 1 minute. The radius of the circle is 70/22 m. Find

I.   instantaneous speed and instantaneous velocity
II.   the average speed,
III.   average velocity in 10 s of motion.

Solution

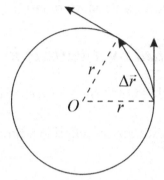

I.   Because of uniform or constant speed, instantaneous and average speed will be equal $\therefore$ Instantaneous speed = magnitude of instantaneous velocity = Average speed.

II. $\therefore$ $\quad v_{inst.} = \dfrac{2\pi r}{T} = \dfrac{2 \times \dfrac{22}{7} \times \dfrac{70}{22}}{60} m/s = \dfrac{1}{3} ms^{-1}$

III.   In 10s the particle completes one sixth of revolution, therefore, $\left| \Delta \vec{r} \right| = r$.

IV. $\left| \vec{v}_{av} \right| = \dfrac{\Delta \vec{r}}{\Delta t} = \dfrac{70}{22} \times \dfrac{1}{10} m/s = \dfrac{7}{22} m/s$ and $\vec{v}_{av}$ makes 120 degree with initial position

vector.

V. $Average \ Speed = \dfrac{\dfrac{\pi r}{3}}{10} m/s = \dfrac{22}{7} \times \dfrac{70}{22} \times \dfrac{1}{30} m/s = \dfrac{1}{3} m/s = constant$

VI.   Note $\dfrac{\Delta r}{\Delta t} = 0$ for this complete motion.

Acceleration

The rate of change of velocity with respect to time is called acceleration. The direction of acceleration vector is that along which the change in velocity takes place.

Average Acceleration

It is defined as the change in velocity in a given time divided by that time. It is a vector quantity; its direction is that of the $\Delta\vec{v}$. Average Acceleration $= \dfrac{\Delta\vec{v}}{\Delta t} = \dfrac{\vec{v}_2 - \vec{v}_1}{t_2 - t_1}$

Thus,

$$\overrightarrow{a_{av}} = \frac{\overline{\Delta v}}{\Delta t} = \frac{\Delta v_x}{\Delta t}\hat{i} + \frac{\Delta v_y}{\Delta t}\hat{j} + \frac{\Delta v_z}{\Delta t}\hat{k}$$

$\dfrac{\Delta v_x}{\Delta t} = \left(a_{av}\right)_x = x$ component of Average Acceleration

$\dfrac{\Delta v_y}{\Delta t} = \left(a_{av}\right)_y = y$ component of Average Acceleration

$\dfrac{\Delta v_z}{\Delta t} = \left(a_{av}\right)_z = z$ component of Average Acceleration

$$a = \left|\vec{a}_{av}\right| = \sqrt{\left(\frac{\Delta v_x}{\Delta t}\right)^2 + \left(\frac{\Delta v_y}{\Delta t}\right)^2 + \left(\frac{\Delta v_z}{\Delta t}\right)^2}$$

CAUTION

The quantities $\dfrac{\Delta v}{\Delta t}$ and $\left|\dfrac{\Delta\vec{v}}{\Delta t}\right|$ are entirely different quantities, that is, $\dfrac{\Delta v}{\Delta t} \neq \left|\dfrac{\Delta\vec{v}}{\Delta t}\right|$. For example, in uniform circular motion the rate of change of speed is zero, i.e., $\dfrac{\Delta v}{\Delta t} = 0$, but $\left|\dfrac{\Delta\vec{v}}{\Delta t}\right| \neq 0$ for many intervals of time.

Exercise 3

A particle is executing circular motion with a constant speed so that time period of revolution is 1 minute. The radius of the circle is 70/22 m. Find average acceleration in 10s of motion.
Solution

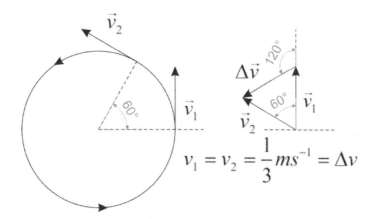

$$v_1 = v_2 = \frac{1}{3}\,ms^{-1} = \Delta v$$

Because of uniform or constant speed, instantaneous speed will be same at both the instants,

$$\therefore \qquad v_1 = v_2$$

$$\therefore \qquad v_1 = v_2 = v_{inst.} = \frac{2\pi r}{T} = \frac{2 \times \frac{22}{7} \times \frac{70}{22}}{60} m/s = \frac{1}{3} ms^{-1}$$

In 10 seconds, the particle covers 1/6 of the circle, therefore, angle between $\vec{v}_1$ & $\vec{v}_2$ is 60^0

$$\therefore \qquad \left| \overline{\Delta v} \right| = v_1 = v_2 = \frac{1}{3} ms^{-1}$$

$$\therefore \qquad \left| \vec{a}_{av} \right| = \frac{\left| \overline{\Delta v} \right|}{\Delta t} = \frac{\frac{1}{3} ms^{-1}}{10 s} = \frac{1}{30} ms^{-2}$$

The direction of average acceleration makes 120^0 with the direction of $\vec{v}_1$.

Instantaneous Acceleration

Suppose a particle undergoes a change in velocity $\overline{\Delta v}$ from time t to $t + \Delta t$. Its average

acceleration during this time is given by $\overrightarrow{a_{av}} = \frac{\overline{\Delta v}}{\Delta t}$. This average acceleration will become the

instantaneous acceleration at time t as the time interval Δt becomes infinitely small i.e., $\Delta t \rightarrow 0$.

Thus, instantaneous acceleration at time t is given by $\vec{a} = \lim_{\Delta t \rightarrow 0} \left(\overrightarrow{a_{av}} \right) = \lim_{\Delta t \rightarrow 0} \left(\frac{\overline{\Delta v}}{\Delta t} \right)$ but

differentiation of velocity vector with respect to time is equal to $\lim_{\Delta t \rightarrow 0} \left(\frac{\overline{\Delta v}}{\Delta t} \right) = \frac{\vec{dv}}{dt}$

Therefore, instantaneous acceleration, $\vec{a} = \frac{\vec{dv}}{dt}$

Writing $\vec{v} = v_x \hat{i} + v_y \hat{j} + v_z \hat{k}$, we get, $\vec{a} = \frac{dv_x}{dt} \hat{i} + \frac{dv_y}{dt} \hat{j} + \frac{dv_z}{dt} \hat{k}$

Also $\vec{a} = a_x \hat{i} + a_y \hat{j} + a_z \hat{k}$

Where $a_x = \frac{dv_x}{dt}, a_y = \frac{dv_y}{dt}$ and $a_z = \frac{dv_z}{dt}$

Since $\vec{v} = \frac{\vec{dr}}{dt}$ therefore, $\vec{a} = \frac{d^2 \vec{r}}{dt^2}$

That is, acceleration is 2nd order time derivative of position vector. In terms of x, y and z components.

$$a_x = \frac{d^2 x}{dt^2}, a_y = \frac{d^2 y}{dt^2} \text{ and } a_z = \frac{d^2 z}{dt^2}$$

Thus, $\vec{a} = \frac{\vec{dv}}{dt} = \frac{dv_x}{dt} \hat{i} + \frac{dv_y}{dt} \hat{j} + \frac{dv_z}{dt} \hat{k} = \frac{d^2 \vec{r}}{dt^2} = \frac{d^2 x}{dt^2} \hat{i} + \frac{d^2 y}{dt^2} \hat{j} + \frac{d^2 z}{dt^2} \hat{k}$

CAUTION

$a = |\vec{a}| = \left|\dfrac{d\vec{v}}{dt}\right| \neq \dfrac{dv}{dt}$, only in straight line motion $a = |\vec{a}| = \left|\dfrac{d\vec{v}}{dt}\right| = \dfrac{dv}{dt}$. It must carefully be noted

that $\left|\dfrac{d\vec{v}}{dt}\right|$ & $\dfrac{dv}{dt}$ are entirely different quantities. There are many situations like that of uniform

circular motion in which $\dfrac{dv}{dt} = 0$ but $\left|\dfrac{d\vec{v}}{dt}\right| = a$ is a finite quantity equal to magnitude of

instantaneous acceleration. Further, it must be noted that $\dfrac{dv}{dt}$ is the rate of change of speed, and

therefore it is the component of acceleration in the direction of velocity vector, it is called tangential acceleration.

Tangential and Normal Acceleration

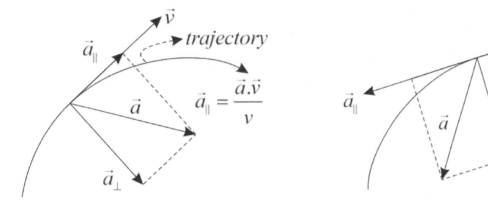

Figure a, speeding up motion   Figure b, slowing down motion

The component of acceleration in the direction of $\vec{v}$, which is $\dfrac{dv}{dt}$, is called tangential acceleration

$\vec{a}_{II}$ and the component of acceleration perpendicular to is called normal acceleration $\vec{a}_{\perp}$. It is the tangential acceleration which is responsible for either speeding up or slowing down the motion, on the other
hand it is the normal acceleration which is responsible for changing the direction of the velocity. The

motion is sped-up, that is, $\dfrac{dv}{dt}$ is positive when tangential acceleration is in the direction of $\vec{v}$ as

shown above in figure a, and the motion is retarded, that is, $\dfrac{dv}{dt}$ is negative when tangential

acceleration is opposite to $\vec{v}$ as shown above in figure b.

Further $\quad a_{II} = \dfrac{\vec{a}.\vec{v}}{v}$ and $\vec{a}_{\perp} = \vec{a} - \vec{a}_{II}$, therefore, $a_{\perp} = \sqrt{a^2 - a_{II}^2}$

Exercise 4

A particle is moving in x-y plane. At a particular instant of time its velocity is $\vec{v} = \left(3\hat{i} + 4\hat{j}\right) ms^{-1}$. At this instant of time, its acceleration is $\vec{a} = \left(5\hat{i}\right) ms^{-2}$. Find the tangential and normal acceleration at this time.

Solution

As, the tangential acceleration, $a_{II} = \dfrac{\vec{a}.\vec{v}}{v}$,

$a_{II} = \dfrac{15}{5} ms^{-2} = 3 ms^{-2}$

and, the normal acceleration, $a_{\perp} = \sqrt{a^2 - a_{II}^2} = \left(\sqrt{25-9}\right) ms^{-2} = 4 ms^{-2}$

Exercise 5

A particle is moving in x-y plane along a parabola $y = \left(2m^{-1}\right) x^2$ with its x co-ordinate depending upon time as $x = \left(1 ms^{-1}\right) t$. Find its tangential and normal acceleration at the moment when it crosses origin.

Solution

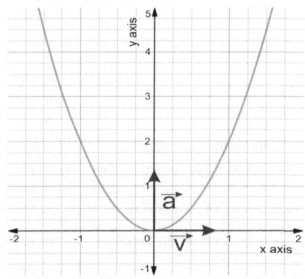

Substitute the value of x in $y = \left(2m^{-1}\right) x^2$, we get $y = \left(2 ms^{-2}\right) t^2$

I. $\quad \vec{r} = \left(1 ms^{-1}\right) t\,\hat{i} + \left(2 ms^{-2}\right) t^2\,\hat{j}$ ... The position vector of the particle

II. $\quad \vec{v} = \dfrac{d\vec{r}}{dt} = \left(1 ms^{-1}\right)\hat{i} + \left(4 ms^{-2}\right) t\,\hat{j}$ ... The velocity vector of the particle

III. $\quad \vec{a} = \dfrac{d\vec{v}}{dt} = \left(4 ms^{-2}\right)\hat{j}$ ... The acceleration vector of the particle

IV. $\quad a_{II} = \dfrac{\vec{a}.\vec{v}}{v} = \dfrac{\left\{\left(1ms^{-1}\right)\hat{i} + \left(4ms^{-2}\right)t\,\hat{j}\right\}.\left(4ms^{-2}\right)\hat{j}}{\sqrt{1m^2s^{-2} + \left(16m^2s^{-4}\right)t^2}} = \dfrac{\left(16m^2s^{-4}\,t\right)}{\sqrt{1m^2s^{-2} + \left(16m^2s^{-4}\right)t^2}}$

...Tangential acceleration of the particle, when the particle is at origin, x = 0 m t = 0s, therefore,
$a_{II} = 0\,ms^{-2}$

V. $\qquad a_{\perp} = \sqrt{a^2 - a_{II}^2}$ $\qquad\qquad\qquad$ ...Normal Acceleration

$\therefore \qquad a_{\perp} = \left(\sqrt{16 - 0}\right)ms^{-2} = 4\,ms^{-2}$

Further, using equations II, III, IV and V, normal and tangential accelerations at any point of the trajectory can be found.

Exercise 6

A balloon is rising vertically up from ground with constant vertical velocity v_o. A horizontal wind causes the balloon to gather horizontal velocity given by $v_x = by$ where y is height above ground and b is a constant. Find the total, tangential and normal acceleration of the balloon as well as horizontal drift & trajectory of the balloon.

Solution

I. $\qquad$ In this problem, vertical velocity v_o is constant i.e., $v_y = \dfrac{dy}{dt} = v_0 = $ constant

II. $\qquad\qquad\qquad v_x = \dfrac{dx}{dt} = by$

III. $\quad\therefore\qquad\qquad \vec{v} = b\,y\,\hat{i} + v_0\hat{j}$

IV. $\qquad$ Therefore, **total acceleration** equals to $\vec{a} = \dfrac{d\vec{v}}{dt} = b\dfrac{dy}{dt}\hat{i} = bv_0\,\hat{i}$

V. $\qquad$ But **tangential acceleration** equals to $a_{II} = \dfrac{\vec{a}.\vec{v}}{v}$

$\therefore \qquad\qquad a_{II} = \dfrac{\left(b\,y\,\hat{i} + v_0\hat{j}\right).\left(bv_0\,\hat{i}\right)}{\sqrt{b^2y^2 + v_0^2}} = \dfrac{b^2v_0\,y}{\sqrt{b^2y^2 + v_0^2}}$

VI. $\qquad$ And the **normal acceleration** equals to $a_{\perp} = \sqrt{a^2 - a_{II}^2}$

$\therefore \qquad a_{\perp} = \sqrt{b^2v_0^2 - \dfrac{b^4v_0^2y^2}{b^2y^2 + v_0^2}} = \sqrt{\dfrac{b^4v_0^2y^2 + b^2v_0^4 - b^4v_0^2y^2}{b^2y^2 + v_0^2}} = \dfrac{bv_0^2}{\sqrt{b^2y^2 + v_0^2}}$

Calculation of Horizontal Drift

From equation I., $dy = v_o dt$

After integration $y = v_o t$

II.   From equation II., $\dfrac{dx}{dt} = by = bv_o t$

$\Rightarrow$ $dx = (bv_o t)dt$

III.   After integration $x = \dfrac{bv_0 t^2}{2} = \dfrac{bv_0}{2}\left(\dfrac{y}{v_0}\right)^2$ or $x = \dfrac{by^2}{2v_0}$

Trajectory of Balloon

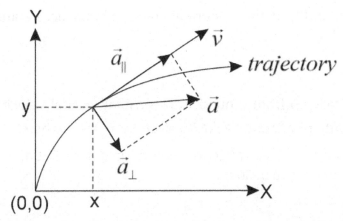

From statement VIII., it is clear that the trajectory of balloon is parabolic. It is shown in the above figure.

KINEMATICAL GRAPHS

A graph between any two physical quantities y and x offers the best method of understanding their dependence on each other. The slope of the graph at any value of x, $\frac{dy}{dx}(=\tan\theta)$, gives the rate of change of y with respect to x at that value of x. The graph offers an insight to understand how does the rate of change of y with respect to x, that is $\frac{dy}{dx}(=\tan\theta)$, vary with x. Apart from this, the area under the graph offers valuable information about the total change in the value of a physical quantity Q whose rate of change with respect to x is the quantity y itself, i.e.,

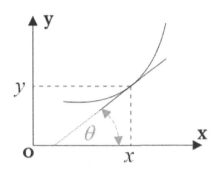 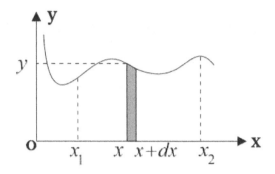

If, $\frac{dQ}{dx}=y$, then $dQ=ydx$,

and so, $\quad \Delta Q = Q_2 - Q_1 = \int_{x_1}^{x_2} ydx =$ Area under y-x graph between x_1 and x_2

Some important kinematical graphs for a particle moving along a straight line

Position (x) - Time (t) graph

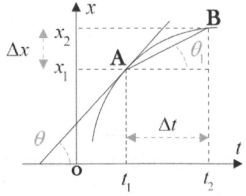

Following information can be obtained from the graph

Average rate of change of position (x) with respect to time (t), which is the average velocity of the particle from time t_1 to t_2 is given by the slope of the chord joining points A $\left(x_1,t_1\right)$ and B $\left(x_2,t_2\right)$.

$$v_{av} = \frac{\Delta x}{\Delta t} = \tan\theta_1$$

Instantaneous velocity at time t_1 is given by the slope of the tangent drawn at point A$\left(x_1,t_1\right)$

$$v = \frac{dx}{dt} = \tan\theta$$

If the position time graph is a straight line, it means its slope, that is, velocity is constant and we conclude the motion is a uniform straight line motion. If the position time graph is a parabola given by $x = A + Bt + Ct^2$, it means its slope, that is, its velocity is changing uniformly with time which indicates that the acceleration of the particle, $\frac{dv}{dt} = 2C$, is constant. Following graphs are to demonstrate the same

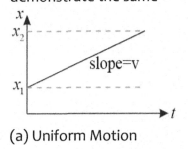

(a) Uniform Motion

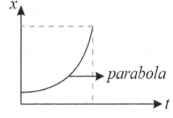

b) Uniformly Accelerated

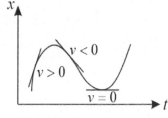

(c) Non-Uniformly Accelerated

Velocity(v) -Time(t) graph

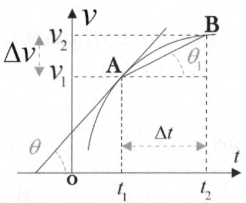

Following information can be obtained from the graph:
Average rate of change of velocity (V) with respect to time (t), which is the average acceleration of the particle from time t_1 to t_2 is given by the slope of the chord joining points A$\left(v_1,t_1\right)$ and B$\left(v_2,t_2\right)$

$$a_{av} = \frac{\Delta v}{\Delta t} = \tan\theta_1$$

Instantaneous acceleration at time t_1 is given by the slope of the tangent drawn at point A$\left(v_1,t_1\right)$

$$a = \frac{dv}{dt} = \tan\theta$$

If the velocity time graph is a straight line parallel to time axis, it means its slope is zero, that is, velocity is constant and we conclude the motion is a uniform straight line motion. If the velocity time graph is an inclined straight line, it means its slope, that is, acceleration is constant and we conclude the motion is a uniformly accelerated straight line motion.

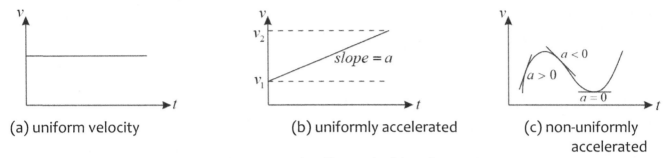

(a) uniform velocity   (b) uniformly accelerated   (c) non-uniformly accelerated

Apart from this, the area under the v-t graph offers valuable information about the total change in the position x, that is displacement of the particle,

As $\dfrac{dx}{dt} = v$, $dx = vdt$

So, $\Delta x = x_2 - x_1 = \displaystyle\int_{t_1}^{t_2} vdt =$ area under the v-t graph between t_1 and t_2

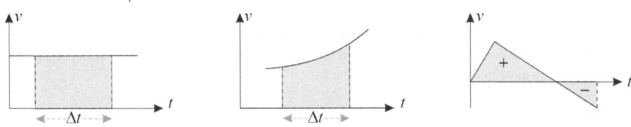

While finding displacement using v-t graph, area under v-t graph is taken negative when velocity is negative. But if we want to determine the distance travelled by the particle, the absolute value of area under v-t graph is taken.

Acceleration (a) -Time(t) graph

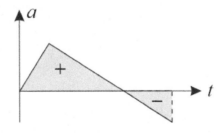

Slope of a-t graph doesn't represent any physical quantity but the area under the a-t graph offers valuable information about the total change in the velocity of the particle and that is $\dfrac{dv}{dt} = a$,

therefore, $dv = adt$

And $\Delta v = v_2 - v_1 = \displaystyle\int_{t_1}^{t_2} adt =$ Area under a-t graph between t_1 and t_2 .

Area under a-t graph is taken negative when acceleration is negative.
Note
Velocity of a particle goes on increasing until acceleration becomes zero. Velocity decreases only when the acceleration changes its sign, that is, when it becomes opposite to the velocity. When the acceleration is continuously in the direction of velocity, velocity goes on increasing no matter if the acceleration is decreasing or if it is constant or increasing. Velocity will be maximum, that is, it will increase no more when the speeding up acceleration has decreased to zero.

Exercise 7

Which of the following graphs indicate maximum change in the velocity of the particle in the time interval T?

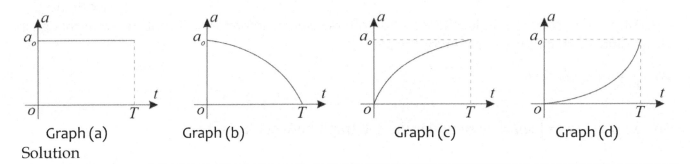

| Graph (a) | Graph (b) | Graph (c) | Graph (d) |

Solution

We know that the change in velocity is indicated by the area under acceleration time graph. As the area under acceleration time graph is maximum in case of graph (a), it is this graph which indicates maximum change in velocity in the shown time interval T.

Exercise 8

A particle starting from rest has variable acceleration along a fixed direction as shown in the following graph. Find the maximum velocity of the particle.

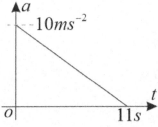

Solution

The velocity will go on increasing until the acceleration is zero. It means the particle will have maximum speed at time t = 11s. But area under a-t graph is the change in velocity, so

$$v_{max} - 0 = \text{Area under the graph} = \frac{1}{2} \times 10 \times 11 \, ms^{-1}$$

$$\Rightarrow v_{max} = 55 \, ms^{-1}$$

Graphs for uniform straight line motion

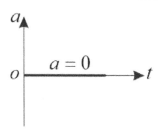

For uniform motion, $a = 0$, v is constant, and $x = x_0 + vt$, therefore various graphs are as follow

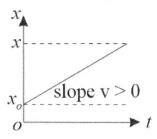
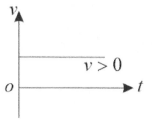

(a) when the particle is moving along positive direction

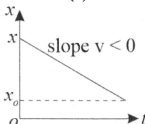
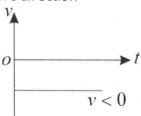

(b) when the particle is moving along negative direction

Graphs for Uniformly Accelerated Straight Line Motion

(a) When the acceleration is along the direction of initial velocity (positive direction) $a(= \text{constant}) > 0$, $v = u + at$ and $x = x_0 + ut + \frac{1}{2}at^2$

various graphs are as follow

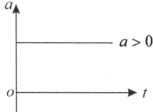
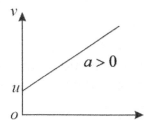
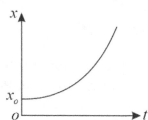

(b) When the acceleration is opposite to initial velocity (negative direction) $a(= \text{constant}) < 0$, $v = u - |a|t$ and $x = x_0 + ut - \frac{1}{2}|a|t^2$

various graphs are as follow

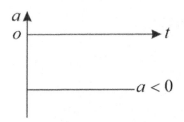
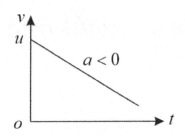
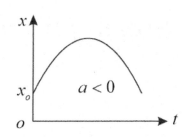

Exercise 9

A ball is dropped from a height h. It strikes ground elastically and rebounds back to the same height. Taking downward direction as positive and initial position to be origin, plot acceleration time (a-t), velocity time (v-t) and position time (x-t) graphs for the round trip journey. Neglect the duration of collision and effect of air.

Solution

This is the case of uniformly accelerated motion where acceleration $a = g =$ constant. For the downward journey, the velocity goes on increasing in positive direction and the slope of v-t graph is $a = g =$ constant. The ball strikes ground with some positive velocity. Immediately after collision with ground the velocity becomes negative having same magnitude as it had just before the collision. For the upward journey, the negative velocity goes on decreasing until it becomes zero at the end of round trip, the slope of v-t graph is again $a = g =$ constant. The position time (x-t) graph consists of two parabolas, one for downward motion with increasing positive slope and the other for upward motion with decreasing negative slope. The graphs are as follow

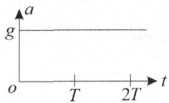
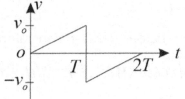
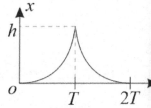

According to these graphs, $T = \sqrt{\dfrac{2h}{g}}$ is the time of free fall from a height h and $v_0 = \sqrt{2gh}$ is the velocity of free fall from that height.

Exercise 10

The velocity time graphs of three cars a, b and c are shown as under with all the three cars seen at origin at t = 0. Plot their acceleration time (a-t) and position time (x-t) graphs.

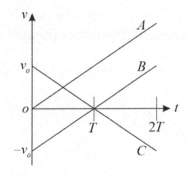

Solution

As the absolute values of slopes of all the three v-t graphs are $\dfrac{v_0}{T}$, therefore the absolute values of accelerations of all the three cars are same equal to $a_0 = \dfrac{v_0}{T}$. Cars A and B have positive accelerations whereas car C has negative acceleration, all are uniformly accelerated.

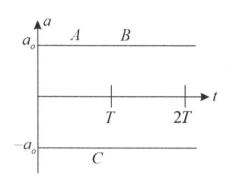

Figure (a) shows the a-t graphs

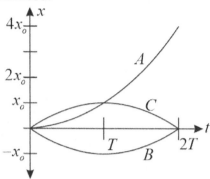

Figure (b) shows the x-t graphs

Further, the absolute values of the displacements of all these three cars in time T are also same, equal to area under v-t graphs $\left(x_0 = \dfrac{v_0 T}{2} \right)$. Cars B and C return to origin in time 2T as the initial velocity of each of them is opposite to acceleration, but car A goes along same direction and undergoes a displacement equal to in this time. All the three x-t graphs are parabolic having following properties

I.   A has zero velocity at t = 0 so slope of x-t graph is zero at this time
II.   B has negative velocity at t = 0 so slope of x-t graph is negative at this time
III.   C has positive velocity at t = 0 so slope of x-t graph is positive at this time
IV.   Both B and C have zero velocity at t = T so the slope of their x-t graphs are zero at this time
V.   Both A and C have same velocity at t = T/2 so the slope of their x-t graphs are same at this time.

GENERAL KINEMATICAL STUDY FOR ALL CASES

We start our kinematical study from some information about acceleration. Let the acceleration of a particle be $\vec{a} = a_x\hat{i} + a_y\hat{j} + a_z\hat{k}$, now we proceed as follows

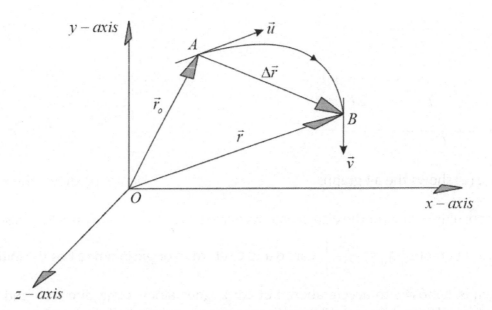

Suppose the initial position and velocity of the particle (at zero time) are $\vec{r}_0$ and $\vec{u}$ these are given by

$$\vec{r}_0 = x_0\hat{i} + y_0\hat{j} + z_0\hat{k} \qquad \text{and} \qquad \vec{u} = u_x\hat{i} + u_y\hat{j} + u_z\hat{k}$$

Here, $\left(x_0, y_0, z_0\right)$ are initial position coordinates and u_x, u_y and u_z are the x, y and z components of initial velocity of the particle. After time t, let the position and velocity of the particle become $\vec{r}$ and $\vec{v}$, then

$$\vec{r} = x\hat{i} + y\hat{j} + z\hat{k} \qquad \text{and} \qquad \vec{v} = v_x\hat{i} + v_y\hat{j} + v_z\hat{k}$$

Here, (x, y, z) are the position coordinates and v_x, v_y and v_z are the x, y and z components of velocity of the particle at time t.

As we know that $\vec{a} = \dfrac{d\vec{v}}{dt} \Rightarrow d\vec{v} = \vec{a}\,dt$, integrating it from t = 0 to t = t, we get

$\displaystyle\int_{\vec{u}}^{\vec{v}} d\vec{v} = \int_{0}^{t} \vec{a}\,dt$, which gives $\vec{v} - \vec{u} = \displaystyle\int_{0}^{t}\vec{a}\,dt$, that is,

I.a. $\qquad \vec{v} = \vec{u} + \displaystyle\int_{0}^{t}\vec{a}\,dt$

Resolving it into rectangular components, we get

I.b.
$$v_x = u_x + \int_0^t a_x dt$$

I.c.
$$v_y = u_y + \int_0^t a_y dt$$

I.d.
$$v_z = u_z + \int_0^t a_z dt$$

From the above set of equations, we can calculate the velocity of the particle at any time.

Now, $\vec{v} = \dfrac{d\vec{r}}{dt}$ $\Rightarrow d\vec{r} = \vec{v}dt$, integrating it from t = 0 to t = t gives

$$\int_{\vec{r}_0}^{\vec{r}} d\vec{r} = \int_0^t \vec{v}dt \qquad \Rightarrow \vec{r} - \vec{r}_0 = \int_0^t \vec{v}\, dt$$

Or
$$\vec{r} - \vec{r}_0 = \int_0^t \left(\vec{u} + \int_0^t \vec{a}dt \right) dt$$

II.a.
Or $\vec{r} - \vec{r}_0 = \vec{u}t + \int_0^t \left(\int_0^t \vec{a}dt \right) dt$

Resolving into rectangular components

II.b.
$$x - x_0 = u_x t + \int_0^t \left(\int_0^t a_x dt \right) dt \qquad \text{or} \qquad x = x_0 + u_x t + \int_0^t \left(\int_0^t a_x dt \right) dt$$

II.c.
$$y - y_0 = u_y t + \int_0^t \left(\int_0^t a_y dt \right) dt \qquad \text{or} \qquad y = y_0 + u_y t + \int_0^t \left(\int_0^t a_y dt \right) dt$$

II.d.
$$z - z_0 = u_z t + \int_0^t \left(\int_0^t a_z dt \right) dt \qquad \text{or} \qquad z = z_0 + u_z t + \int_0^t \left(\int_0^t a_z dt \right) dt$$

From the above set of equations, we can calculate the position of the particle at any time.

By eliminating time from equations II.b, II.c and II.d we get a relationship between the x, y and z coordinates of the particle, that is, we get the equation of trajectory of the particle.

The shape of trajectory is given by the over-all picture of how velocity bends every time from the start of motion up to the time of observation.

As we know that the velocity bends every time in the direction of acceleration, therefore, the shape of the trajectory is determined by the way the pair, $\vec{v}\ and\ \vec{a}$ changes. If $\vec{v}\ and\ \vec{a}$ remain in same plane, the trajectory is planar and the motion is at most two-dimensional. For a motion to be three-dimensional, the plane containing $\vec{v}\ and\ \vec{a}$ must keep on changing with time, for which the first condition is that the acceleration must be non-uniform.

Special Case of Uniformly Accelerated Motion

If the acceleration is constant i.e., $\vec{a}$ is constant, then the equations under set number **I.** change into

III. $\vec{v} = \vec{u} + \vec{a}t$, $v_x = u_x + a_x t$, $v_y = u_y + a_y t$ and $v_z = u_z + a_z t$

And the equations under set number 2 change into

IV. $\vec{r} - \vec{r}_0 = \vec{u}t + \dfrac{\vec{a}t^2}{2}$, $x - x_0 = u_x t + \dfrac{a_x t^2}{2}$, $y - y_0 = u_y t + \dfrac{a_y t^2}{2}$ and $z - z_0 = u_z t + \dfrac{a_z t^2}{2}$

But when the acceleration is constant the plane containing initial velocity $\vec{u}$ and the acceleration vector $\vec{a}$ remains the plane that contains $\vec{v}$ and $\vec{a}$ vectors for all times and therefore the trajectory will be a planar trajectory. Therefore, taking the plane of $\vec{u}$ and $\vec{a}$ as x-y plane, we see $a_z = 0$, $u_z = 0$, so, from equations **III.** and **IV.** it is clear that there is no kinematical quantity along z-direction and the motion is confined to x-y plane. In x-direction, the velocity-time and position- time relations are as follow

V. $v_x = u_x + a_x t$

VI. $x - x_0 = u_x t + \dfrac{a_x t^2}{2}$

And in y-direction, the velocity-time and position-time relations are

VII. $v_y = u_y + a_y t$

VIII. $y - y_0 = u_y t + \dfrac{a_y t^2}{2}$

Further in such a case, as the direction of acceleration is fixed, we choose the direction of acceleration to be one of the two mutually perpendicular directions out of x and y. Let us take x -direction to be along acceleration, we write $\vec{a} = a\hat{i}$ which gives $a_x = a$ and $a_y = 0$.

By doing so the equations **VI.**, **VII.** and **VIII.** turn into

A. $v_y = u_y$

B. $y - y_0 = u_y t$

C. $v_x = u_x + at$

D. $x - x_0 = u_x t + \dfrac{1}{2} at^2$

Using these equations, the study of the motion becomes very simplified. In this situation if initial velocity is along x-direction, i.e., $u_y = 0$ then the motion is along x-direction only and we get uniformly accelerated straight line motion.

UNIFORMLY ACCELERATED STRAIGHT LINE MOTION

In case of uniformly accelerated straight line motion, if the particle is supposed to move along x-direction and x_0 is the position of the particle at zero time and $u_x = u$ is its initial velocity

then its velocity at any time is given by

I. $\qquad v = u + at$

and its position x, at this time t, is given by

II. $\qquad x - x_0 = ut + \dfrac{1}{2}at^2$

By eliminating t between equations, **I.** & **II.** we get,

III. $\qquad v^2 - u^2 = 2a\left(x - x_0\right)$

By writing $\left(x - x_0\right) = S$, equations **II.** & **III.** can also be written as

$$S = ut + \frac{1}{2}at^2 \text{ and } v^2 - u^2 = 2aS$$

Following important features of this type of motion are note-worthy.

Graphs for uniformly accelerated straight line motion

(a) when the acceleration is along the direction of initial velocity (positive direction), $a(= \text{constant}) > 0$, $v = u + at$ and $x = x_0 + ut + \dfrac{1}{2}at^2$, so various graphs are as follow

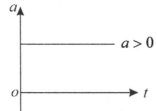 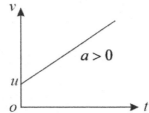 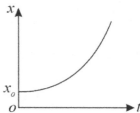

(b) when the acceleration is opposite to initial velocity (negative direction), $a(= \text{constant}) < 0$, $v = u - at$ and $x = x_0 + ut - \dfrac{1}{2}at^2$, so various graphs are as follow

 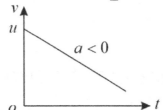 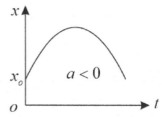

Displacement of a uniformly accelerated object in n^{th} second of its motion

The displacement in n^{th} second of motion (represented by S_{nth}) is the displacement from time $(n-1)$ second to n seconds of time

$$S_{nth} = \int_{n-1}^{n} (u + at)\,dt = \left[ut + \frac{1}{2}at^2 \right]_{n-1}^{n}$$

or

$$S_{nth} = u\{n - (n-1)\} + \frac{a}{2}\{n^2 - (n-1)^2\}$$

or

$$S_{nth} = u + \frac{a}{2}(2n - 1)$$

Displacement of a uniformly retarded object in last second of its motion

If n^{th} second be the last second of motion, that is, that second in which the object stops, then from $v = u + at$, putting v = 0 and replacing a with $-a$ and t by n, we get,
$0 = u - an$ giving n = u /a

So,

$$S_{nth} = S_{Last} = u - \frac{a}{2}\left(\frac{2u}{a} - 1\right) = \frac{a}{2}$$

Galilean Relation

When a uniformly accelerated particle starts from rest then its displacement in equal successive intervals of time is calculated as follows

Displacement in first time interval:

$$\Delta x_{1st} = \frac{1}{2}a(\Delta t)^2$$

Displacement in second time interval:

$$\Delta x_{2nd} = \frac{1}{2}a(2\Delta t)^2 - \frac{1}{2}a(\Delta t)^2 = \frac{3}{2}a(\Delta t)^2$$

Displacement in third time interval:

$$\Delta x_{3rd} = \frac{1}{2}a(3\Delta t)^2 - \frac{1}{2}a(2\Delta t)^2 = \frac{5}{2}a(\Delta t)^2$$

Displacement in fourth time interval:

$$\Delta x_{4th} = \frac{1}{2}a(4\Delta t)^2 - \frac{1}{2}a(3\Delta t)^2 = \frac{7}{2}a(\Delta t)^2$$

Thus, we obtain the relation $\Delta x_{1st} : \Delta x_{2nd} : \Delta x_{3rd} : \Delta x_{4th} \ldots = 1 : 3 : 5 : 7 \ldots$
Above relation is called Galilean relation.

Distance and displacement relation

If the initial velocity is in the same direction as that of the acceleration, then distance travelled remains equal to the displacement for all intervals of time, but the two quantities may be different if the motion is a retarding one (that is, when initial velocity is opposite to the acceleration). In such cases of retarded- motion the particle stops after some and then it turns to travel in the direction of acceleration for the rest of the time. So, the distance travelled remains equal to the displacement only for those intervals of time which do not include the turning event of the particle.

Exercise 11

A particle starts with 50 m/s to move along a straight line with uniform retardation of $10ms^{-2}$. Find the distance covered and displacement of the particle in 6 seconds of motion.
Solution

As it is the case of a retarded motion, firstly we must assure if the time given includes the turning event or not.
Let t be the time after which the particle turns back, i.e., t is the time at which the particle stops for a while, then from $v = u + at$, putting v = 0 and replacing a with $-10ms^{-2}$ and u with 50 m/s , we get,

$0 = 50m/s - \left(10ms^{-2}\right)t \Rightarrow$ t = 5s. This shows that the time given includes the turning event so, the

distance and displacement of the particle in 6 seconds of motion will be different.

Displacement, $\Delta x = ut + \frac{1}{2}at^2 = \left(50 \times 6 - 5 \times 36\right)m = 120m$

For calculating distance covered in 6 seconds, we calculate the absolute values of its displacements (that is, distance travelled) in first 5 seconds and in one second after 5th second separately and then we add them.

Distance covered in 5 seconds $= \Delta x_5 = ut + \frac{1}{2}at^2 = \left(50 \times 5 - 5 \times 25\right)m = 125m$

Distance covered in one second from 5th second to 6th second is calculated as follows

$$\left|\Delta x_{5-6}\right| = \left|ut + \frac{1}{2}at^2\right| = \left|0 - 5 \times 1^2\right|m = 5m$$

Thus, the distance travelled in 6s = 125m + 5m = 130m.

An example of Uniformly accelerated straight line motion

Motion Under Gravity in Vertical Straight Line

If the effect of air is neglected, the motion of an object thrown vertically upward or vertically downward is purely under gravity. In this case, if the motion extends only up to those heights which are much smaller than the radius of earth, the acceleration is fairly uniform and equals to g (= 9.8 m/s²) vertically downwards. Consider such a case in which a small object (a stone or a ball) is thrown vertically upwards from ground with initial velocity u_0. As the upward journey is retarded because of downward acceleration g, the ball stops after reaching a certain height H above ground. After that it starts falling down with zero initial velocity and strikes ground with velocity v_{back}, (magnitude of v_{back} will be proved to be equal to that of u_o).

Let us denote upward direction to be positive y-direction.

Therefore, $\vec{a} = -g\,\hat{j}$ and so $a = a_y = -g$

Further, let us identify upward journey by I and downward journey by II.

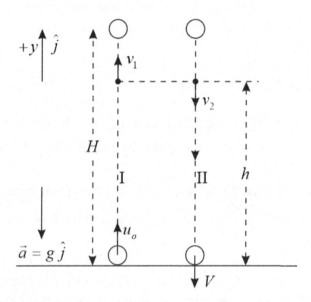

I.   Time of Flight(T)

In this time, finally the displacement of object $\Delta y = 0$

$u = u_o$, $a = -g$ and $t = T_1$ then from $s = ut + \dfrac{1}{2}at^2$, $\quad 0 = u_0 T - \dfrac{1}{2}gT^2$

I. $\Rightarrow T = \dfrac{2u_0}{g}$

II.   Time of Rise (T_1)

In this time, final velocity $v = 0$

$u = u_o$, $a = -g$, $t = T_1$, then from $v = u + at$, $\quad 0 = u_0 - gT$

II. $\Rightarrow T_1 = \dfrac{u_0}{g}$

III.   Time of fall (T_2)

III. $$T_2 = T - T_1 = \dfrac{2u_0}{g} - \dfrac{u_0}{g} = \dfrac{u_0}{g}$$

i.e., $T_2 = T_1$. This shows time of rise is equal to time of fall.

IV. Maximum height (H) reached

At maximum height final velocity $v = 0$

using $\quad v^2 - u^2 = 2aS$

$\Rightarrow \qquad 0 - u_0^2 = 2(-g)H$

IV. $\qquad\qquad\qquad\qquad H = \dfrac{u_0^2}{2g}$

V. Striking back Velocity

To find it we will use, $v^2 - u^2 = 2aS \quad v = 0 \quad S = h$

For the whole round trip journey put $v = v_{back}$, $u = u_0$, $a = -g$ and $s = 0$

we get, $\qquad v_{back}^2 - u_0^2 = 0 \Rightarrow v_{back}^2 = u_0^2$

V. $\qquad\qquad\qquad\qquad v_{back} = -u_0$

negative sign shows it is directed downward. It is clear that the object strikes back the ground with the same speed with which it was thrown upwards.

VI. Two instants (t_1 and t_2) for same height above ground

There are two such moments when the particle is at same height above ground, one during upward journey and second during downward journey. Let h be the value of height, then using

$S = ut + \dfrac{1}{2}at^2$

$$h = u_0 T - \dfrac{1}{2}gT^2$$

$\Rightarrow \qquad\qquad gT^2 - 2h = 2u_0 T$

$\Rightarrow \qquad\qquad t = \dfrac{2u_0 \pm \sqrt{4u_0^2 - 8gh}}{2g}$

$\Rightarrow \qquad\qquad t_1 = \dfrac{u_0 - \sqrt{u_0^2 - 2gh}}{g} \qquad\qquad$ during upward journey

and $\qquad\qquad t_2 = \dfrac{u_0 + \sqrt{u_0^2 - 2gh}}{g} \qquad\qquad$ during downward journey

therefore, $\qquad\qquad t_1 - t_2 = \dfrac{2\sqrt{u_0^2 - 2gh}}{g}$

and $\qquad\qquad t_1 + t_2 = \dfrac{2u_0}{g} = T \qquad$ which is equal to total time of flight

also
$$t_1t_2 = \frac{2h}{g}$$

Velocities 1 and 2 at these instants

Using, $v^2 - u^2 = 2aS$ and putting $u = u_0$, $S = h$ and $a = -g$, we get

$$v^2 - u^2 = -2gh$$

$\Rightarrow \qquad v^2 = u^2 - 2gh$

$\Rightarrow \qquad v = \pm\sqrt{u_0^2 - 2gh}$

$\Rightarrow \qquad v = +\sqrt{u_0^2 - 2gh} \qquad\qquad$ during upward journey

and $\qquad v = -\sqrt{u_0^2 - 2gh} \qquad\qquad$ during downward journey

It is clear that the speeds $\left|v_1\right|$ and $\left|v_2\right|$ are same.

That is, the object crosses the same point above ground with same speed both during upward and downward journey.

Exercise 12

A flight balloon is rising up with constant velocity of 10 ms⁻¹. When it is at a height of 40 meters above ground, a food packet is dropped from it, find the time taken by it to reach ground. Take g = 10 m/s².
Solution

Considering upward direction positive, we have for the total journey

$$a = -g, \; u = +10ms^{-1}, \; S = -40m$$

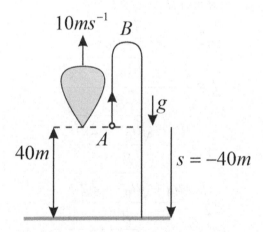

Using $S = ut + \frac{1}{2}at^2$,

$$-40m = 10t - \frac{10}{2}t^2$$

$\Rightarrow \qquad -40m = 10t - 5t^2$

$\Rightarrow \qquad t^2 - 2t - 8 = 0$

$$\Rightarrow \qquad t = \frac{2 \pm \sqrt{4+32}}{2} s$$

$$\Rightarrow \qquad t = \frac{2+6}{2} s = 4s$$

Exercise 13

From the top of a 100 m high cliff, a ball is dropped. At the same moment another ball is thrown vertically upwards with initial speed of 50 m/s directly towards first ball. Find when and where the two balls collide. Take g = 10 m/s².

Solution

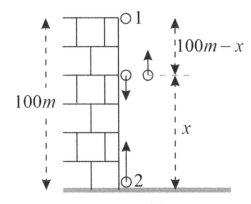

Let us assume that the two balls collide at a height x above ground at time t after it was thrown.

Motion of ball 1, $\qquad a = -g$, $u = 0$, $S = -(100m - x)$, $\qquad$ using $S = ut + \frac{1}{2} at^2$

I. $$-(100m - x) = -\frac{1}{2} gt^2 \text{ or } 100m - x = \frac{1}{2} gt^2$$

Motion of ball 2, $\qquad u = +50ms^{-1}$, $S = +x$, $a = -g$

using $$S = ut + \frac{1}{2} at^2$$

II. $$x = (50ms^{-1})t - \frac{1}{2} gt^2$$

Adding equations I. and II., yields, $100m = (50ms^{-1})t$

$$\Rightarrow \qquad t = 2s$$

put $t = 2s$ and $g = 10ms^{-2}$ in equation II. we get,

$$x = 100m - \frac{1}{2} \times 10 \times 4m = 80m$$

$$\Rightarrow \qquad x = 80m$$

Thus, the two balls collide 80m above ground and 2 seconds after they are thrown.

Exercise 14

From the top of a 45 m high cliff a stone is dropped. 1 second after another stone is thrown vertically downward with such a speed that both the stones reach ground simultaneously. Find the speed with which second stone was thrown. Take g = 10 m/s²

Solution

Taking downward direction as positive direction, we have

For 1st stone

$$u=0,\ a=g=10ms^{-2},\ S=+45m$$

Using
$$S=ut+\frac{1}{2}at^2$$

$$45=5t^2 \Rightarrow t=3s$$

For 2nd Stone

Time of flight of 2nd stone t' is given by $t'=3s-1s=2s$.

Using
$$S=ut+\frac{1}{2}at^2$$

$$45=2u+5\times4$$

$$\Rightarrow \qquad 2u=25ms^{-1}\ or\ u=12.5ms^{-1}$$

Exercise 15

A stone thrown vertically upwards passes across a vertical 5 ft high window. If its total up and down time across the window is 1 sec, find how much high does it rise above the window (g = 32 ft s⁻².)

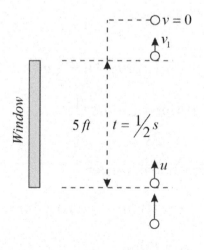

Solution

As   time of fall = time of rise

$$\text{total time across window} = 1s = 2 \times (\text{time of rise})$$

$$\text{time of rise across window} = \frac{1}{2}s$$

Let the velocity the stone when it arrives at the bottom of the window is u and that when it just crosses the top of the window is v_1.

Using $S = ut + \frac{1}{2}at^2$ and substituting, $t = \frac{1}{2}s$, $a = -g = -32\,ft\,s^{-2}$ and $S = 5\,ft$

we get

$$5\,ft = u(\tfrac{1}{2}s) - \frac{1}{2}(32\,ft\,s^{-2})(\tfrac{1}{2}s)^2$$

giving

$$5 = \frac{u}{2} - 4$$

or

$$u = 18\,ft\,s^{-1}$$

Further, using

$$v = u + at$$

$$v_1 = \left[18 - 32 \times \frac{1}{2}\right]ft\,s^{-1}$$

$$v_1 = 2\,ft\,s^{-1}$$

If the stone rises to a height of h above the window

then using $v^2 - u^2 = 2aS$ and substituting $v = 0$, $u = 2\,ft\,s^{-1}$ and $S = h$,

we get

$$0 - 4 = 2(-32)h$$

or

$$h = \frac{1}{16}\,ft$$

Exercise 16

A flight balloon is rising vertically upwards with constant velocity of 10 m/s. When it is at a height of 45 meter above ground, a parachutist bails out of it. The parachute takes 3s in opening up. A retardation of 5 m/s² starts acting on the parachutist after that. Find

I.   Distance of parachutist from balloon and from ground at the time parachute opens

II.   The speed with which the parachutist strikes ground

III.   Total time taken by the parachutist from balloon to ground. (Take g = 10 m/s²)

Solution

Before the parachute opens

When the parachutist bails out of the balloon, his velocity is same as that of the balloon, that is, 10 m/s vertically upwards. Suppose he travels d_1 distance downwards before the parachute opens.

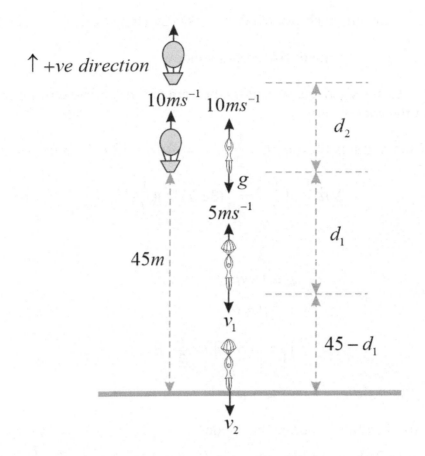

Using

$$S = ut + \frac{1}{2}at^2$$

Substituting $u = 10ms^{-1}$, $S = -d_1$, $a = -g = -10ms^{-2}$ and $t = 3s$

we get

$$-d_1 = 10 \times 3 - 5 \times 9$$

$$d_1 = 15m$$

As the balloon is rising up with constant speed, the upward distance travelled by balloon during this time equals $d_2 = (10 \times 3)m = 30m$

I. Therefore, distance of parachutist from balloon at the time parachute opens is

$$d_1 + d_2 = (30 + 15)m = 45m$$

And at this time the distance of parachutist from ground is $45m - 15m = 30m$.

If v_1 is the velocity of the parachutist at the moment parachute opens then

using

$$v = u + at$$

$$v_1 = 10ms^{-1} - (10ms^{-2})(3s)$$

we get

$$v_1 = 20ms^{-1}$$

negative sign shows the parachutist is falling downward.

After the parachute opens up

The parachutist has to travel a distance of 45 m – 15 m = 30 m downward after the opening of parachute. If V_2 is his velocity with which he falls on ground then, using

$$v^2 - u^2 = 2aS$$

substituting
$$v = v_2, \ u = v_1 = -20 ms^{-1}$$

$$a = +5 ms^{-2}, \ S = -30m,$$

we get
$$v_2^2 - 400 = 10 \times (-30)$$

$$v_2^2 = \left(100 ms^{-1}\right)^2$$

II.
$$v_2 = 50 ms^{-1}$$

negative sign is taken because he is falling downward.

If t_2 is the time between opening of parachute and striking ground then

using
$$v = u + at$$

$$-10 ms^{-1} = -20 ms^{-1} + \left(5 ms^{-2}\right) t_2$$

$\Rightarrow$
$$t_2 = 2s$$

III. $\therefore$ Total time between bailing out & striking the ground $= (3+2)s = 5s$

Exercise 17

A ball is thrown up. If air resistance is taken into consideration and supposed to be a constant force F against motion of ball, compare time of rise & time of fall.

Solution

For upward journey

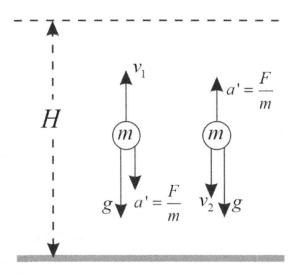

The net-downward acceleration equals $a = g + a'$

If u_0 is the speed of throw and $T_1 =$ Rise time

then using

$$v = u + at$$

$$0 = u_0 - (g + a')T$$

$$\Rightarrow \qquad T_1 = \frac{u_0}{g + a'} = \frac{u_0}{g + \dfrac{F}{m}}$$

If the ball rises up to H, then using $v^2 - u^2 = 2aS$

$$0 - u_0^2 = -2(g + a')H$$

$$\Rightarrow \qquad H = \frac{u_0^2}{2(g + a')} = \frac{u_0^2}{2\left(g + \dfrac{F}{m}\right)}$$

For downward journey

Net downward acceleration is $\qquad a = g - a' = g - \dfrac{F}{m}$

Therefore, if T_2 is the time of fall then using $\qquad S = ut + \dfrac{1}{2}at^2$

$$-H = 0 - \frac{1}{2}(g - a')T_2^2$$

$$\Rightarrow \qquad T_2^2 = \frac{2H}{(g - a')}$$

$$\Rightarrow \qquad T_2 = \frac{u_0}{\sqrt{g^2 - a'^2}} = \frac{u_0}{\sqrt{g^2 - \left(\dfrac{F}{m}\right)^2}}$$

Thus, Rise Time $\qquad T_1 = \dfrac{u_0}{(g + a')}$

Fall Time $\qquad T_2 = \dfrac{u_0}{\sqrt{g^2 - a'^2}}$

Clearly $\qquad T_2 > T_1 \qquad$ (Fall Time > Rise Time)

Exercise 18

To measure the human reaction time or response time of a boy, a meter scale is suddenly made to fall through the loose gap between the thumb and fore finger of the boy's hand. Before the boy catches it, it slips down a distance of 19.6 cm. Find his reaction time.

Solution

Let the reaction time of boy be t, using $\qquad S = ut + \dfrac{1}{2}at^2$

Substituting $S = 19.6 \times 10^{-2} m$, $a = 9.8 ms^{-2}$ and $u = 0$

We get $\qquad \dfrac{19.6}{100} = \dfrac{9.8}{2} t^2 \qquad \Rightarrow t^2 = \dfrac{19.6}{100 \times 4.9} s^2 \qquad \Rightarrow \quad t = \dfrac{2}{10} s = 0.2 s$

EXEMPLAR EXERCISES ON STRAIGHT LINE MOTION

Exercise 19

The maximum retardation of some car that it's brakes-tires-road system can produce is 4.5 m/s². The reaction time of the car driver is 0.2s. Find the safe-driving speed on a busy city road on which the car has to be stopped with in a distance of 28m to avoid accident.

Solution

The driver will be able to apply brakes only after the passage of 0.2s. During this, the car goes on with constant velocity. Let the initial speed (Driving speed) of the car be u.

Distance travelled by the car before the application of brakes

$$S_2 = ut$$

$$S_1 = u \, (0.2s)$$

The remaining distance is $28m - u \, (0.2s)$, if the car takes S₂ distance before stops then

I. $\qquad\qquad (S_2)_{max} = 28m - u \, (0.2s)$

Now using $\qquad\qquad v^2 - u^2 = 2aS$

Substituting $v = 0$, $a = -4.5 ms^{-1}$, $S = (S_2)_{max}$ and $u = u$ we get

II. $\qquad\qquad (S_2)_{max} = \dfrac{u^2}{9}$

From I. and II. $\qquad \dfrac{u^2}{9} = 28 - 0.2u$

III. Or $\qquad\qquad \dfrac{u^2}{9} + u \, (0.2) - 28 = 0$

Finding the roots of equation III.

$$\dfrac{u^2}{9} + u \, (0.2) - 28 = 0$$

$$\Rightarrow \quad \frac{u^2}{9}+\frac{u}{5}-28=0 \quad \Rightarrow \quad u=\frac{-\frac{1}{5}\pm\sqrt{\frac{1}{25}+\frac{4\times28}{9}}}{\frac{2}{9}} \quad \Rightarrow \quad u=\frac{-\frac{1}{5}\pm\frac{1}{15}\sqrt{9+2800}}{\frac{2}{9}}$$

$$\Rightarrow \quad u=\frac{-\frac{1}{5}\pm\frac{1}{15}\sqrt{2809}}{\frac{2}{9}}$$

Considering the positive root of the equation,

$$u=-\frac{9}{10}+\frac{9}{30}\times53=\frac{9}{10}\left[\frac{53}{3}-1\right]=\frac{9}{10}\times\frac{50}{3}=15$$

Thus
$$u=15ms^{-1}=54km\,h^{-1}$$

Exercise 20

A point moving with constant acceleration from A to B in the straight line AB has velocities u and v at A and B respectively. Find its velocity at C, the mid-point of AB. Also, if the time taken to travel from A to C is twice of time taken from C to B then show that v = 7 u.

Solution

Let the particle move with a constant acceleration 'a' and at point A its velocity be u while at point B its velocity be v. Let the distance between A and B be S, then   I.

$$v^2-u^2=2aS$$

Let v_1 be the velocity of the point C, then ∵ distance AC = $\frac{S}{2}$

∴
$$v_1^2=u^2+2a\frac{S}{2}$$

II. or
$$2v_1^2=2u^2+2aS$$

Subtracting equations I. from II., we have $2v_1^2=v^2+u^2$

III. or
$$v_1=\sqrt{\left(\frac{v^2+u^2}{2}\right)}$$

Let t be the time taken to travel from C to B. As time taken to travel from A to C is twice of what is taken from C to B, therefore, time taken to travel from A to C is 2t. Thus, total time of travel between A and B is 3t.

Using $v=u+at$, from A to C, we get

IV.
$$v_1=u+a(2t)$$

Using $v=u+at$, from C to B, we get

V.
$$v=v_1+at$$

Subtracting 2 times **II.** from **I.** gives

VI. $$3v_1 = u + 2v$$

Substituting the value of v_1 in equation **VI.** from equation **III.**

we get $$u + 2v = 3\sqrt{\left(\frac{v^2 + u^2}{2}\right)}$$

Squaring and solving above equation gives us

$$u^2 + 4v^2 + 4uv = \frac{9u^2 + 9v^2}{2}$$

or $$v^2 - 8uv + 7u^2 = 0$$

$\Rightarrow$ $$v(v - 7u) - u(v - 7u) = 0$$

$\Rightarrow$ $$(v - u)(v - 7u) = 0$$

But $$(v - u) \neq 0$$

$$(v - 7u) = 0$$

$\Rightarrow$ $$v = 7u$$

Exercise 21

A car starts moving rectilinearly, first with acceleration a = 5.0 m/s² (the initial velocity is equal to zero), then uniformly, and finally, decelerating at the same rate a, comes to a stop. The total time of motion equals T = 25s. The average velocity during that time is equal to $\overline{V}$ = 72 km per hour. How long does the car move uniformly?

Solution

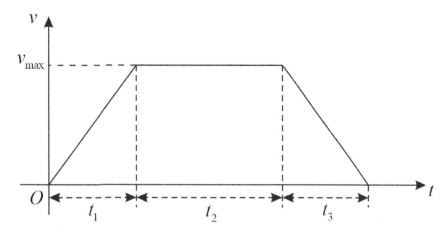

The distances travelled during acceleration and during deceleration are equal and the times $t_1 = t_3$ and therefore, $t_2 = 25s - 2t_1$

From the definition of average velocity

$$\bar{v} = \frac{displacement}{time}$$

Total displacement = average velocity time taken$= 20 \ ms^{-1} \times 25 \ s = 500 \ m$

From the graph   *Total displacement* $= v_{max} \ t_1 + v_{max} \left(25s - 2t_1 \right)$

I. $v_{max} \ t_1 + v_{max} \left(25s - 2t_1 \right) = 500m$

But $\dfrac{v_{max}}{t_1} = 5ms^{-2} \Rightarrow v_{max} = 5t_1$

Equation I. becomes $5t_1^2 + 5t_1 \left(25s - 2t_1 \right) = 500$

$$t_1^2 - 25t_1 + 100 = 0$$

$$t_1 = 5s$$

$$t_2 = 25s - 2t_1 = 15s$$

Exercise 22

A particle beginning from rest, travels a distance S with uniform acceleration and immediately after travels a distance of 3 S with uniform speed followed by a distance 5 S with uniform deceleration, and comes to rest. Find the ratio of average speed to the maximum speed of the particle.

Solution

Let us assume that *the maximum speed* $= v_{max}$, *total time of acceleration* $= t_1$,

total time with uniform velocity $= t_2$ and *total time of deceleration* $= t_3$

We know that, *Area under the v − t curve = total displacement*

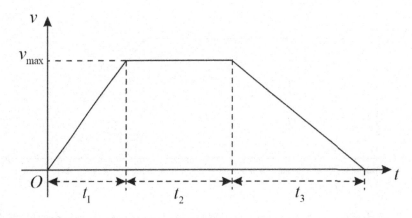

From graph, $S = \dfrac{v_{max}t_1}{2}$, $3S = v_{max}t_2$ and $5S = \dfrac{v_{max}t_3}{2}$

∴ $v_{max} \ (t_1 + t_2 + t_3) = 2S + 3S + 10S = 15S$

Now average speed, $\bar{v} = \dfrac{S + 3S + 5S}{t_1 + t_2 + t_3} \Rightarrow \bar{v}(t_1 + t_2 + t_3) = 9S$

Hence required ratio, $\dfrac{\bar{v}}{v_{max}} = \dfrac{9S}{15S} = \dfrac{3}{5}$

Two Special Cases of Average Speed

Let v_1 and v_2 be the speeds for the two parts of path of length x_1 and x_2 and t_1 and t_2 are the times taken to cover these parts, then $t_1 = \dfrac{x_1}{v_1}$ and $t_2 = \dfrac{x_2}{v_2}$

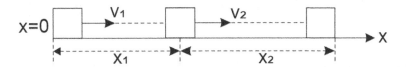

Therefore,

I.
$$v_{av} = \dfrac{x_1 + x_2}{t_1 + t_2} = \dfrac{x_1 + x_2}{\dfrac{x_1}{v_1} + \dfrac{x_2}{v_2}}$$

When two halves of the path are covered with two constant different speeds

In this case substituting $x_1 = x_2 = x$ in equation I. yields

$$v_{av} = \dfrac{2v_1 v_2}{v_1 + v_2} \qquad \text{(Harmonic mean of two speeds)}$$

When two parts of the path are covered in equal times

In this case substituting $t_1 = t_2 = t$, $x_1 = v_1 t$ and $x_2 = v_2 t$ in equation I. yields

$$v_{av} = \dfrac{v_1 + v_2}{2} \qquad \text{(Arithmetic mean of two speeds)}$$

UNIFORMLY ACCELERATED TWO DIMENSIONAL MOTION

A very good example of uniformly accelerated two dimensional motion is projectile motion under gravity, let us study the kinematics of such motion

Projectile motion under constant gravity

I.   A Projectile Thrown at an Angle θ with Horizontal to Fall Back on Ground

Consider a projectile thrown with speed u from ground, the velocity vector $\vec{u}$ making an angle θ with the horizontal. It is obvious that if there is no consideration of air and wind, the motion of the projectile will be in a vertical plane (the plane of $\vec{u}\ and\ \vec{a}$). As the only accelerating agency is the force of gravity, if we assume it be constant, the acceleration of the projectile, throughout its motion, will be uniform equal to g vertically downward, the acceleration due to gravity (g).

Thus, the motion of the projectile will be a two dimensional uniformly accelerated motion. Let us denote this two-dimensional vertical plane to be x-y plane, selecting horizontal direction as x-direction and vertically upward direction as y-direction.

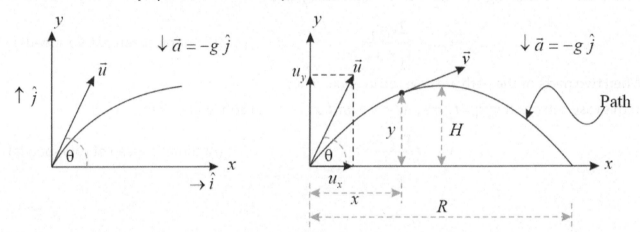

Resolving the initial velocity and acceleration in two mutually perpendicular x and y directions, we get

$$u_x = u\cos\theta, u_y = u\sin\theta , a_x = 0 \text{ and } a_y = -g$$

As the projectile advances far and far in horizontal direction, it moves up and down in vertical direction also. Therefore, the shape of the path i.e., trajectory appears like that is shown in the figure given above. Consider, the origin to be the point from where the projectile is shown. Let at an instant of time t, its co-ordinates are (x, y) and its velocity is $\vec{v} = v_x\hat{i} + v_y\hat{j}$. At this time, the horizontal displacement of the projectile is $\Delta x = x - 0$ and its velocity in horizontal direction is v_x.

And, at this time, its vertical displacement is $\Delta y = y - 0$ and vertical velocity is v_y. As both the motions, the motion in x-direction and simultaneous motion in y-direction are independent we can study them independently as two uniformly accelerated one-dimensional motions having common time.

Motion in x-direction

$u_x = u \cos\theta$, $a_x = 0$ and $\Delta x = x - 0 = x$

The equation, $\qquad v_x = u_x + a_x t \qquad$ gives,

I. $\qquad\qquad v_x = u \cos\theta$

And the equation, $\qquad \Delta x = u_x t + \dfrac{1}{2} a_x t^2 \qquad$ gives,

II. $\qquad\qquad x = \Delta x = (u \cos\theta) t$

Motion in y-direction

$u_y = u \sin\theta$, $a_y = -g$ and $\Delta y = y - 0 = y$

The equation, $\qquad v_y = u_y + a_y t \qquad$ gives,

III. $\qquad\qquad v_y = u \sin\theta - gt$

And the equation, $\qquad \Delta y = u_y t + \dfrac{1}{2} a_y t^2 \qquad$ gives,

IV. $\qquad\qquad y = \Delta y = (u \sin\theta) t - \dfrac{1}{2} gt^2$

Also, the equation, $\quad v_y^{\,2} - u_y^{\,2} = 2 a_y \Delta y \quad$ gives,

V. $\qquad\qquad v_y^{\,2} - u^2 \sin^2\theta = -2gy$

That is, we can study the complete motion by the following simultaneous equations

For x-direction

I. $\qquad\qquad v_x = u \cos\theta$

II. $\qquad\qquad x = \Delta x = (u \cos\theta) t$

and for y-direction

III. $\qquad\qquad v_y = u \sin\theta - gt$

IV. $\qquad\qquad y = \Delta y = (u \sin\theta) t - \dfrac{1}{2} gt^2$

V. $\qquad\qquad v_y^{\,2} - u^2 \sin^2\theta = -2gy$

1. The Time of Flight (T)

It is total time for which the projectile remains above ground. That is, it is the time taken, between the point of throw and point of strike by the projectile. Obviously, when the projectile is back on the ground to strike (or hit) it, its vertical displacement at this moment is zero. Thus, the time of flight can be obtained from equation **IV.** by substituting $\Delta y = 0$ in it. We get,

$$(u \sin \theta)t - \frac{1}{2}gt^2 = 0$$

or

$$t\left[u \sin \theta - \frac{1}{2}gt\right] = 0$$

giving

$$t = 0 \text{ and } t = \frac{2u \sin \theta}{g}$$

Here $t = 0$, is the time (or instant) when the projectile was thrown and $t = \frac{2u \sin \theta}{g}$ is the time when the projectile falls back on the ground. Therefore, the total time of flight comes out to be as follows

VI.

$$T = \frac{2u \sin \theta}{g} = \frac{2u_y}{|a_y|}$$

2. Horizontal Range (R)

It is the total horizontal displacement of the projectile between the point of throw and point of hit. Obviously, it is the amount of Δx in a time, $t = T = \frac{2u \sin \theta}{g}$. Thus, we get the horizontal range (R) by substituting $t = \frac{2u \sin \theta}{g}$ in equation **II.**, we obtain the following relationships

$$R = (u \cos \theta).\frac{2u \sin \theta}{g}$$

Therefore,

$$R = \frac{u^2 2 \sin \theta.\cos \theta}{g}$$

VII.   Or

$$R = \frac{u^2 \sin 2\theta}{g} = \frac{2u_x u_y}{|a_y|}$$

3. Maximum Height Attained (H)

The projectile will rise up only up to a point where its vertical velocity (v_y) becomes zero. The vertical displacement up to this point is the maximum Height (H) that the projectile will attain above ground. We get

it from equation **V.** by putting $v_y = 0$, $y = y = H$. Thus,

$$0 - u^2 \sin^2 \theta = -2gh \quad \text{giving}$$

VIII.

$$H = \frac{u^2 \sin^2 \theta}{2g} = \frac{u_y^2}{2|a_y|}$$

4. Shape of the Path (Trajectory)

The shape of the path will be determined by the mathematical relationship between x & y co-ordinates. We do so by eliminating time (t) from

equations **II.** and **IV.** From equation **II.**, $t = \dfrac{x}{u\cos\theta}$, substituting it in equation **IV.**, we get,

$$y = (u\sin\theta)\left(\frac{x}{u\cos\theta}\right) - \frac{g}{2}\cdot\frac{x^2}{u^2\cos^2\theta}$$

IX.   or

$$y = (\tan\theta)x + \left(\frac{-g}{2u^2\cos^2\theta}\right)x^2$$

which is of the form $y = Ax + Bx^2$

where $A = \tan\theta = $ some constant value

and $B = \dfrac{-g}{2u^2\cos^2\theta} = $ some constant value

Since, it is the equation of a parabola therefore, the shape of the path of the projectile is parabolic. The equation of trajectory, equation **IX.**, can also be written as follows

X.

$$y = x\tan\theta\left(1 - \frac{x}{R}\right)$$

5. Maximum Value of Horizontal Range for a Given Speed of Projection (u)

The horizontal range of a projectile for a given speed of projection is: $R = \dfrac{u^2\sin 2\theta}{g}$, clearly it will be maximum when $\sin 2\theta$ is maximum. But the maximum value of $\sin 2\theta$ is 1, therefore, the maximum horizontal range is $R_{\max} = \dfrac{u^2}{g}$. This will happen (i.e., $\sin 2\theta$, becomes equal to 1) only when $2\theta = 90°$ or when $\theta = 45°$. Thus, the projectile will possess (or will cover) maximum horizontal range when it is thrown in a direction making an angle of 45° with the horizontal and the maximum value of the range will be $\dfrac{u^2}{g}$.

6. Two Angles of Projection for a Given Range at a Given Speed of Projection

If the projectile is thrown making an angle θ with the horizontal, the range of the projectile is

I.

$$R_1 = \frac{u^2\sin 2\theta}{g}$$

If we throw it at an angle 90° – θ with the horizontal, its range will be

$$R_2 = \frac{u^2 \sin 2(90° - \theta)}{g} = \frac{u^2 \sin(180° - 2\theta)}{g}$$

II.   or

$$R_2 = \frac{u^2 \sin 2\theta}{g}$$

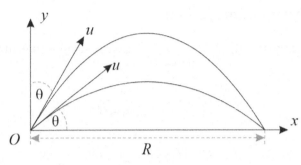

Comparing **I.** and **II.**, we get $R_1 = R_2$

Thus, if we project a projectile at an angle x or at an angle 90° – θ, the range will be same. We may visualize it in another way also. As the range is $R = \dfrac{2u_x u_y}{\left| a_y \right|}$, so by changing θ to 90° – θ,

u_x and u_y interchange their values and their product remains unchanged hence the value of range remains same at both of these angles which are complementary to each other.

7.   Projectile Thrown to Attain Maximum Height as High as Possible

Maximum height attained $H = \dfrac{u^2 \sin^2 \theta}{2g}$

Obviously, the projectile will rise to attain maximum possible value of max. height only if $\sin^2 \theta$ is maximum i.e., $\sin^2 \theta = 1$, therefore, $\theta = \dfrac{\pi}{2}$

i.e., when projectile is thrown vertically upwards.

In that case, $H_{max} = \dfrac{u^2}{2g} = \dfrac{R_{max}}{2}$

Exercise 23

Bheema of Mahabharata could throw his mace as far as 500 meters, how high could he throw it?

Solution

The maximum horizontal range of the mace, $R_{max} = 500m$

Since $R_{max} = \dfrac{u^2}{g}$ therefore, $500m = \dfrac{u^2}{g}$

As the greatest value of the maximum height is $\dfrac{u^2}{g}$,

$$H_{\max} = \dfrac{u^2}{2g} = \dfrac{500}{2}\, m$$

or $$H_{\max} = 250m$$

Thus, Bheema could throw it as high as 250 m.

8. Maximum Height Attained During the Journey When Projectile is Projected for Maximum Horizontal Range

$$R_{\max} = \dfrac{u^2}{g}$$

substitute $\theta = 45°$ in the formula for H i.e., in the following formula

$$H = \dfrac{u^2 \sin^2 \theta}{2g}$$

We get,

$$H = \dfrac{u^2 . \sin^2 45°}{2g} = \dfrac{u^2}{4g}$$

$\Rightarrow$

$$H = \dfrac{R_{\max}}{4}$$

Exercise 24

An athlete throws a stone to go as far as possible. It falls at a distance 80 m away from him. Find, how much high it rises during the journey.

Solution

$$H = \dfrac{R_{\max}}{4} = 20m$$

9. Angle of Throw for Which the Projectile's Maximum Height is n^{th} Part of Horizontal Range

That is,

$$H = \dfrac{R}{n}$$

For that

$$\dfrac{u^2 \sin^2 \theta}{2g} = \dfrac{u^2 \sin 2\theta}{ng}$$

$\Rightarrow$

$$\dfrac{\sin^2 \theta}{2} = \dfrac{2 \sin \theta \cos \theta}{n}$$

$\Rightarrow$

$$\tan \theta = \dfrac{4}{n} \text{ or } \theta = \tan^{-1} \dfrac{4}{n}$$

10. Projectile Passing Through Two Points at Same Height Above Ground

I.
$$y = (u\sin\theta)t - \frac{1}{2}gt^2$$

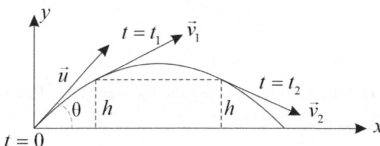

II.
$$v_y = u\sin\theta - gt$$

III.
$$v_y^2 = u^2\sin^2\theta - 2gy$$

Relationship between speeds v_1 and v_2 at such points

IV.
$$v_1 = v_{x_1}\hat{i} + v_{y_1}\hat{j}$$

V.
$$v_2 = v_{x_2}\hat{i} + v_{y_2}\hat{j}$$

We know that $\qquad v_{x_1} = v_{x_2} = u\cos\theta =$ some constant value

For finding v_{y_1} and v_{y_2}, substitute y = h in equation **III.**

$$v_y^2 = u^2\sin^2\theta - 2gh$$

$\Rightarrow$
$$v_y = \pm v_y = \sqrt{u^2\sin^2\theta - 2gh}$$

$\Rightarrow$
$$v_{y_1} = \sqrt{u^2\sin^2\theta - 2gh}$$

And
$$v_{y_2} = \sqrt{u^2\sin^2\theta - 2gh}$$

VI. $\qquad \therefore \qquad \vec{v}_1 = u\cos\theta\,\hat{i} + \left(\sqrt{u^2\sin^2\theta - 2gh}\right)\hat{j} \qquad$ VII.

$\qquad$ And $\qquad \vec{v}_2 = u\cos\theta\,\hat{i} - \left(\sqrt{u^2\sin^2\theta - 2gh}\right)\hat{j}$

$\Rightarrow$
$$v_1 = \sqrt{u^2\cos^2\theta + u^2\sin^2\theta - 2gh}$$

$\Rightarrow$
$$v_1 = \sqrt{u^2 - 2gh}$$

Similarly,
$$v_2 = \sqrt{u^2 - 2gh}$$

This shows $v_1 = v_2$ that is, the projectile has same speed at same height.

Average velocity between these two points

For uniformly accelerated motion

VIII.
$$\vec{v}_{av} = \frac{\vec{v}_1 + \vec{v}_2}{2}$$

Substituting the values of $\vec{v}_1$ and $\vec{v}_2$ from equations **VI.** and **VII.** in equation **VIII.** we get

$$\vec{v}_{av} = (u\cos\theta)\,\hat{i}$$

Time Interval ($t_1 - t_2$) between these points

Substituting y = h in equation **I.**, we get

$$gt^2 - 2(u\sin\theta)t + 2h = 0$$

$$t = \frac{2u\sin\theta \pm \sqrt{4u^2\sin^2\theta - 8gh}}{2g}$$

$$\Rightarrow \qquad t_1 = \frac{u\sin\theta - \sqrt{u^2\sin^2\theta - 2gh}}{g}$$

and
$$t_2 = \frac{u\sin\theta + \sqrt{u^2\sin^2\theta - 2gh}}{g}$$

(i)
$$t_2 - t_1 = \frac{2\sqrt{u^2\sin^2\theta - 2gh}}{g}$$

(ii)
$$t_2 + t_1 = \frac{2u\sin\theta}{g} = T$$

(iii)
$$t_2 t_1 = \frac{2h}{g} \qquad \text{or} \qquad h = \frac{1}{2}g\,t_1 t_2$$

11. Relationship Between Max Heights H_1 And H_2 for Two Projectiles Thrown with Same Speed to Achieve Same Range

For achieving same range, if one projectile is thrown at θ angle with horizontal, the other has to be thrown at $\left(\dfrac{\pi}{2} - \theta\right)$ with the horizontal, two maximum heights are

$$H_1 = \frac{u^2\sin^2\theta}{2g} \quad \text{and} \quad H_2 = \frac{u^2\cos^2\theta}{2g}$$

adding these heights gives $\quad H_1 + H_2 = \dfrac{u^2}{2g} = \dfrac{R_{max}}{2}$

12. The Time When the Projectile Moves Perpendicular to its Initial Velocity

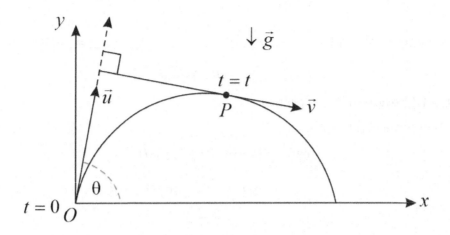

Method (i)

As at this time $\vec{v} = \vec{u} + \vec{g}\,t$ is perpendicular to $\vec{u}$, therefore, their dot product is zero, which gives

$$\left(\vec{u} + \vec{g}\,t\right).\vec{u} = u^2 + t\,\vec{g}.\vec{u} = 0$$

$$\Rightarrow \qquad u^2 + t\,g\,u\cos\left(90 + \theta\right) = 0 \qquad \text{or} \qquad u^2 - t\,g\,u\sin\theta = 0$$

$$\Rightarrow \qquad t = \frac{u}{g\sin\theta}$$

Method (ii)

As $\vec{g}\,t = \vec{v} - \vec{u}$ and $\vec{v} \perp \vec{u}$, therefore, using Pythagoras theorem, we get

$$gt = \sqrt{v^2 + u^2}$$

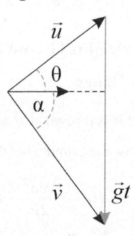

As the horizontal component of velocity does not change $\therefore v\cos\alpha = u\cos\theta$ since $\alpha = 90^0 - \theta$ $\therefore v\sin\theta = u\cos\theta$, that is, $v = u\cot\theta$ and we get

$$gt = \sqrt{u^2\cot^2\theta + u^2}$$

$$\Rightarrow \qquad gt = u\sqrt{\cot^2\theta + 1} \qquad \text{or} \qquad t = \frac{u}{g\sin\theta}$$

Condition for this event to happen

This can happen only if this time is lesser than the total time of flight, i.e.,

$$\frac{u}{g\sin\theta} \le \frac{2u\sin\theta}{g} \qquad \Rightarrow \qquad \sin^2\theta \ge \frac{1}{2} \text{ or } \theta \ge 45^0$$

13. Direction of Motion at Any Point on the Trajectory

If the velocity vector $\vec{v}$ makes angle α with the horizontal at any time then, as the horizontal component of velocity does not change,

$$v\cos\alpha = u\cos\theta$$

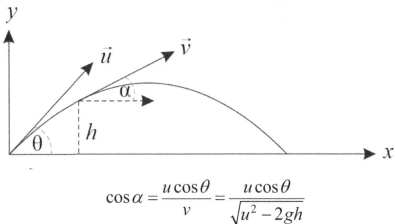

$$\cos\alpha = \frac{u\cos\theta}{v} = \frac{u\cos\theta}{\sqrt{u^2 - 2gh}}$$

Exercise 25

A particle is projected from ground at an angle θ with horizontal with some velocity. For any position A on the trajectory as shown find the relation between the angles α, β and θ.

Solution

In triangle OAM, $\tan\alpha = \dfrac{h}{x}$ and in triangle AMB $\tan\beta = \dfrac{h}{R-x}$,

$$\tan\alpha + \tan\beta = \frac{h}{x} + \frac{h}{R-x}$$

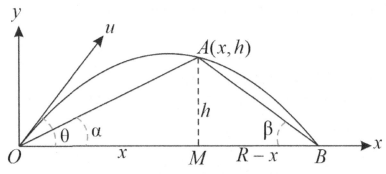

I. or $$\tan\alpha + \tan\beta = \frac{Rh}{x(R-x)}$$

But from the equation of trajectory $y = x\tan\theta\left(1 - \dfrac{x}{R}\right)$, substituting y = h

$$h = x\tan\theta\left(1 - \frac{x}{R}\right)$$

II. $\Rightarrow$

$$\frac{Rh}{x(R-x)} = \tan\theta$$

$\therefore$ from equations **I.** and **II.**, $\tan\alpha + \tan\beta = \tan\theta$, which is the desired relation.

Exercise 26

A goal is attempted by kicking the football from mid-field towards the goal post with providing it a velocity of 64 ft per second at an angle 45^0 above horizontal. 10 ft high, goal post is 120 ft away from the mid-field. Find if the attempt is successful or not. Take $g = 32\,ft/s^2$.

Solution

For the attempt to be successful the horizontal Range of the ball must be greater than 120ft and if this condition is satisfied, it should be at a height lesser than 10 ft when it comes at the position of goal post. That is the conditions are (i) $R > 120\,ft$ and (ii) $y < 10\,ft$ when x = 120ft. Let us see:

I.

$$R = \frac{u^2}{g} = \frac{64 \times 64}{32}\,ft = 128\,ft$$

Thus, $\qquad\qquad R > 120\,ft$

II.   The equation of trajectory is

$$y = x\tan\theta\left(1 - \frac{x}{R}\right) \Rightarrow \qquad y = 120\left(1 - \frac{120}{128}\right)ft$$

$\Rightarrow$

$$y = \frac{120 \times 8}{128}\,ft$$

$\Rightarrow$

$$y = 7.5\,ft$$

Thus, $\qquad\qquad y < 10\,ft$

Hence both the conditions are satisfied and the attempt is successful.

Exercise 27

A hunter aims his gun and fires a bullet directly towards a monkey sitting at a distant tree. At the instant bullet leaves the barrel of the gun, the monkey drops from the tree freely. Will the bullet hit the monkey?

Solution

Suppose the horizontal distance of the tree be D from the hunter and original height, at which the monkey was, be H. The angle of projection will be given by $\tan\theta = \dfrac{H}{D}$

I.   i.e., $D \tan \theta = H$

If the bullet reaches a point under the tree at a height y above ground in time t, suppose it covers a horizontal distance equal to R in that time.

$\therefore$ $$D = (u \cos \theta)t$$

$$t = \frac{D}{u \cos \theta}$$

II. $\therefore$

By using the equation of trajectory, the vertical height of the bullet when it reaches under the tree is

$$y = D \tan \theta - \frac{1}{2} g \left(\frac{D}{u \cos \theta} \right)^2$$

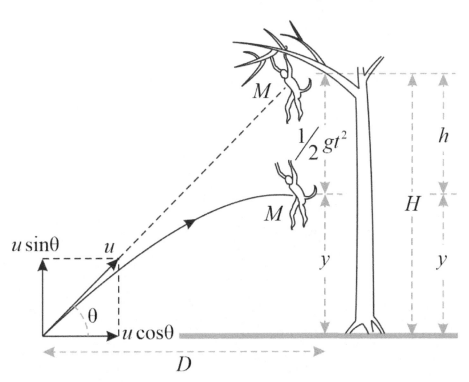

III.   writing $D \tan \theta = H$ $y = H - \frac{1}{2} g \left(\frac{D}{u \cos \theta} \right)^2$

At this time, if the monkey falls down a distance h, then

$$h = \frac{1}{2} g t^2 = \frac{1}{2} g \left(\frac{D}{u \cos \theta} \right)^2$$

If the height of monkey above ground at this time be y', then y' will be given by

$$y' = H - h$$

IV. or $$y' = H - \frac{1}{2}g\left(\frac{D}{u\cos\theta}\right)^2$$

From equation **III.** and **IV.** $y = y'$

This implies that, at the moment the bullet reaches under tree, both monkey and the bullet are at same height above ground. That is, the bullet hits the monkey.

Exercise 28

Two persons simultaneously aim their guns at a bird sitting on a tree. The first person fires his shot with a speed of 100 m/s at an angle of projection of 37°. The second person is ahead of the first by a distance of 50 m and fires his shot with a speed of 75 m/s. How must he aim his gun so that both the shots hit the bird simultaneously? Calculate the distance of the foot of the tree from two persons and the height of the tree. With what velocities and when do the two shots hit the bird?

Solution

The situation in the problem is shown in the figure.

For first shot

Let horizontal displacement = x_1 and Vertical displacement = h

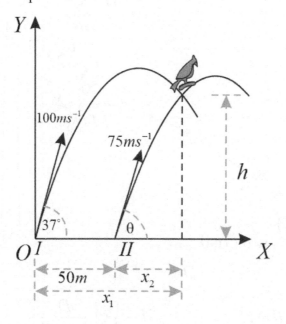

For second shot

Horizontal displacement = x_2 and Vertical displacement = h

I. It is given that $x_1 = x_2 + 50m$

II. For first shot, $h = (100\sin 37°)t - \frac{1}{2}gt^2$

III. For second shot $h = 75(\sin\theta)t - \frac{1}{2}gt^2$

Subtracting II. and III.,
$$75(\sin \theta) = 100 \sin 37°$$

$\Rightarrow$
$$\sin \theta = \frac{100 \sin 37°}{75} = \frac{4}{5}$$

$\Rightarrow$
$$\theta = 53°$$

Now,
$$x_1 = (100 \cos 37°)t$$

and
$$x_2 = 75(\cos 53°)t$$

substituting x_1 and x_2 in equation I. gives

$$(100 \cos 37°)t = 75(\cos 53°)t + 50$$

$\Rightarrow$
$$t[80 - 45] = 50$$

$\Rightarrow$
$$t = \frac{50}{35}s = 1.43s$$

Further,
$$x_1 = (100 \cos 37°) \times \frac{50}{35} m = 114.28\ m$$

And
$$x_2 = (114.28 - 50)m = 64.28\ m$$

Also,
$$h = (100 \sin 37°)\frac{50}{35} m - \frac{1}{2} \times 10 \times \left(\frac{50}{35}\right)^2 m = 75.5\ m$$

Exercise 29

A ball is thrown from ground level so as to just clear a wall 4 m high at a distance of 4 m and falls at a distance of 12 m from the wall. Find the magnitude and direction of the initial velocity of throw.

Solution

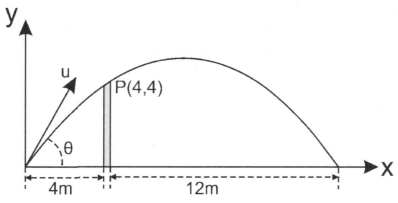

The ball passes through the point P (4,4). So, its range = 4 + 12 = 16 m.

The trajectory of the ball is $\quad y = x \tan \theta \left(1 - \dfrac{x}{R}\right)$

Now $\qquad\qquad\qquad$ x = 4 m, y = 4 m and R = 16m

$$4 = 4\tan\theta\left[1 - \frac{4}{16}\right] = (4\tan\theta).\frac{3}{4}$$

or
$$\tan\theta = \frac{4}{3},\ \theta = 53°$$

$$\sin\theta = \frac{3}{5},\ \cos\theta = \frac{4}{5}$$

Since
$$R = \frac{2u^2\sin\theta\cos\theta}{g}$$

Therefore,
$$16 = \frac{2}{10}\times u^2 \times \frac{4}{5}\times\frac{3}{5}$$

$\Rightarrow$
$$u^2 = \frac{16\times 10\times 25}{2\times 4\times 3} = \frac{500}{3}$$

$\Rightarrow$
$$u = \sqrt{166.7}\ ms^{-1} = 12.9 ms^{-1}$$

Exercise 30

Two particles are projected from a point simultaneously with velocities whose horizontal and vertical components are u_1, v_1 and u_2, v_2 respectively. Prove that the interval between their passing through the other common point of their path is

$$\frac{2(v_1 u_2 - v_2 u_1)}{g(u_1 + u_2)}$$

Solution

We will analyze the following figure to solve the problem. Suppose the two particles pass through the second common point M. Let the two particles starting from 1st common point O take time t₁ and t₂ respectively to pass through the second common point M. Since distances covered by two particles in horizontal directions up to point M will be same, therefore

I.
$$u_1 t_1 = u_2 t_2$$

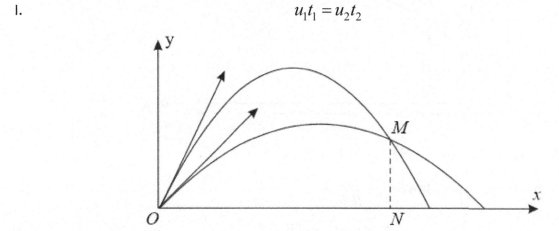

Similarly, in vertical directions also

II.
$$v_1 t_1 - g t_1^2 = MN = v_2 t_2 - g t_2^2$$

From equation **II.** we get
$$t_1^2 - t_2^2 = \frac{2(v_1 t_1 - v_2 t_2)}{g}$$

III. $\Rightarrow$
$$(t_1 + t_2)(t_1 - t_2) = \frac{2(v_1 t_1 - v_2 t_2)}{g}$$

but from equation **I.**
$$\frac{u_1}{u_2} = \frac{t_2}{t_1}$$

$\Rightarrow$
$$\frac{u_1 + u_2}{u_2} = \frac{t_2 + t_1}{t_1}$$

IV. $\Rightarrow$
$$t_1 + t_2 = \frac{(u_1 + u_2)}{u_2} \times t_1$$

From equations, **III.** and **IV.** we get
$$(t_1 - t_2) \times \frac{(u_1 + u_2)}{u_2} \times t_1 = \frac{2}{g}\left(v_1 t_1 - v_2 \frac{u_1}{u_2} \times t_1 \right)$$

$\Rightarrow$
$$(t_1 - t_2) \times \frac{(u_1 + u_2)}{u_2} = \frac{2}{g}\left(v_1 - v_2 \frac{u_1}{u_2} \right)$$

$\Rightarrow$
$$(t_1 - t_2) = \frac{2}{g} \times \frac{u_2}{(u_1 + u_2)} \times \frac{(v_1 u_2 - v_2 u_1)}{u_2}$$

$\Rightarrow$
$$(t_1 - t_2) = \frac{2(v_1 u_2 - v_2 u_1)}{g(u_1 + u_2)}$$

Exercise 31

The radii of the front and rear wheels of a carriage are a and b respectively and c is the distance between their axle-trees. A dust particle driven from the highest point of the rear wheel is observed to land on the highest point of the front wheel. Show that the velocity of the carriage is
$$v = \sqrt{\frac{g(c+b-a)(c-b+a)}{4(b-a)}}$$

Solution

Let the velocity of the carriage be v. The velocity of point A will be twice of the velocity of the carriage. Therefore, the velocity of the dust particle with respect to the carriage will be equal to 2v – v = v.

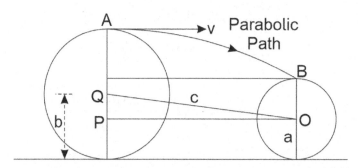

Suppose the highest point of the rear wheel is A and highest point of the front wheel is B. Let v be the velocity of the carriage. The points A and B are at heights 2b and 2a from the ground. The dust particle leaves the highest point A of the rear wheel with linear horizontal velocity v and move along a parabolic path AB to land at the highest point B of front wheel.

Let t be the time of flight along the parabolic arc AB. The horizontal distance between the wheels is,

$$PO = \left[OQ^2 - OP^2 \right]^{\frac{1}{2}} = \left[c^2 - (b - a)^2 \right]^{\frac{1}{2}}$$

But
$$PO = Horizontal\ range\ of\ the\ flight = vt$$

$$vt = \left[c^2 - (b - a)^2 \right]^{\frac{1}{2}}$$

$$\Rightarrow \qquad t = \frac{1}{v} \left[c^2 - (b - a)^2 \right]^{\frac{1}{2}}$$

During this time interval the dust particle falls through a vertical distance $= 2b - 2a = 2(b-a)$ under gravity. Its initial vertical velocity is zero

$$\Rightarrow \quad 2(b-a) = \frac{1}{2}gt^2 \quad \Rightarrow \quad 2(b-a) = \frac{1}{2}g\frac{\left[c^2 - (b-a)^2 \right]}{v^2} \quad \Rightarrow$$

$$v^2 = \frac{g[c^2 - (b-a)^2]}{4(b-a)}$$

$$\Rightarrow \qquad v = \sqrt{\frac{g(c+b-a)(c-b+a)}{4(b-a)}}$$

Exercise 32

One second after the projection, a stone moves at 45^0 with horizontal and two seconds after projection it moves horizontally. Find its angle of projection.

Solution

At time t = 1s, $\qquad\qquad v_y = v_x = u_x = u\cos\theta$

But $v_y = u \sin \theta - gt$

After comparing both equations, we can write

$$u \sin \theta - gt = u \cos \theta$$

I. $\Rightarrow$ $u \sin \theta - 10 = u \cos \theta$

At time t = 2s, $v'_y = u \sin \theta - gt = 0$

II. $\Rightarrow$ $u \sin \theta = 20$

III. From equations, I. and II.,

$$u \cos \theta = 10$$

From equations, II. and III., $\tan \theta = 2$

$\Rightarrow$ $\theta = \tan^{-1} 2$

Exercise 33

Show that the motion of one projectile as seen from another projectile will always be a straight line motion.

Solution

As clearly shown in figure, assume two projectiles to be thrown from the origin O of the XY-plane with velocities u_1 and u_2, making angles θ_1 and θ_2 respectively, with X-axis. After time t, let the two projectiles

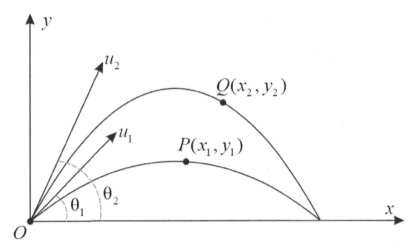

occupy positions P (x_1, y_1) and Q (x_2, y_2). Then,

$$x_1 = u_1 \cos \theta_1 . t$$

And $$y_1 = u_1 \sin \theta_1 . t - \frac{1}{2} gt^2$$

also, $$x_2 = u_2 \cos \theta_2 . t$$

and $$y_2 = u_2 \sin \theta_2 . t - \frac{1}{2} gt^2$$

$$\therefore \quad x_2 - x_1 = (u_2 \cos\theta_2 - u_1 \cos\theta_1)t$$

and

$$y_2 - y_1 = (u_2 \sin\theta_2 - u_1 \sin\theta_1)t$$

$$\therefore \quad \frac{y_2 - y_1}{x_2 - x_1} = \frac{u_2 \sin\theta_2 - u_1 \sin\theta_1}{u_2 \cos\theta_2 - u_1 \cos\theta_1}$$

If (x, y) be the coordinates of point Q relative to the point P, then

$$x_2 - x_1 = x \qquad \text{and} \qquad y_2 - y_1 = y$$

$$\therefore \quad \frac{y}{x} = m \qquad \text{or} \qquad y = mx \qquad \text{(the equation of a straight line)}$$

Hence the motion of a projectile as seen from another projectile is a straight line motion.

II. A Projectile Fired Horizontally from a Certain Height Above Ground

Consider a projectile fired horizontally with a speed u from a height H above ground. Considering the point of throw as origin, horizontal direction as x-direction and vertically downward direction as y-direction, we have: $\vec{a} = g\,\hat{j}$ and $\vec{u} = u\,\hat{i}$ that is, $a_x = 0$, $a_y = g$, $u_x = u$ and $u_y = 0$. Let the projectile be at a point (x, y) at an instant of time t after throw. Its motion in x-direction and simultaneous motion in y-direction can be understood by the following equations:

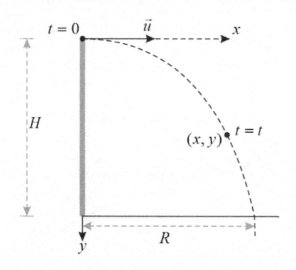

Motion in x-direction

$$u_x = u, \ a_x = 0, \ \Delta x = x - 0 = x$$

using

$$v_x = u_x + a_x t$$

I.   we get

$$v_x = u$$

using

$$\Delta x = x = u_x t + \frac{1}{2} a_x t^2$$

II.   we get

$$\Delta x = x = ut$$

Motion in y-direction

$$u_y = 0, \; a_y = g, \; \Delta y = y - 0 = y$$

using

$$v_y = u_y + a_y t$$

III.   we get

$$v_y = gt$$

and using

$$\Delta y = y = u_y t + \frac{1}{2} a_y t^2$$

IV.   we get

$$\Delta y = y = \frac{g}{2} t^2$$

V.   Also

$$v_y^2 - 0^2 = 2gy$$

1.   Time of flight (t)

It is the total time taken by the projectile to land on the ground after being thrown. Obviously, the moment the projectile hits the ground, the vertical displacement y becomes equal to H. Therefore, from equation **IV.**, we get the time of flight as:

$$H = \frac{g}{2} T^2 \qquad \Rightarrow \qquad T^2 = \frac{2H}{g}$$

VI.

$$T = \sqrt{\frac{2H}{g}}$$

2.   Horizontal range

From equation **II.**, put t = T, the horizontal displacement in this time is the horizontal range R. We get:
$$R = u.T$$

That is,

$$R = u\sqrt{\frac{2H}{g}}$$

3.   Trajectory

From equation **II.** $t = \frac{x}{u}$, substituting in equation **IV.** Gives,

$$y = \frac{g}{2} \frac{x^2}{u^2}$$

that is

$$y = \left(\frac{g}{2u^2} \right) x^2$$

or

$$y = Bx^2$$

where

$$B = \left(\frac{g}{2u^2} \right) \neq 0$$

This is equation of a parabola. Thus, the path is parabolic.

Exercise 34

Two paper screen A and B are separated by a distance of 100m. A bullet pierces A and then B. The hole in B is 10 cm below the hole in A. If the bullet is travelling horizontally at the time of hitting the screen A, calculate the velocity of the bullet when it hits the screen A. Neglect the resistance of paper and air.

Solution

Assume that the bullet hits the screen with velocity u and pierces the screen after time t.

$\therefore$ Horizontal distance, $PQ = R = ut = 100m$ and $H = QR = 0.1m$

$\therefore$ from
$$R = u\sqrt{\frac{2H}{g}}$$

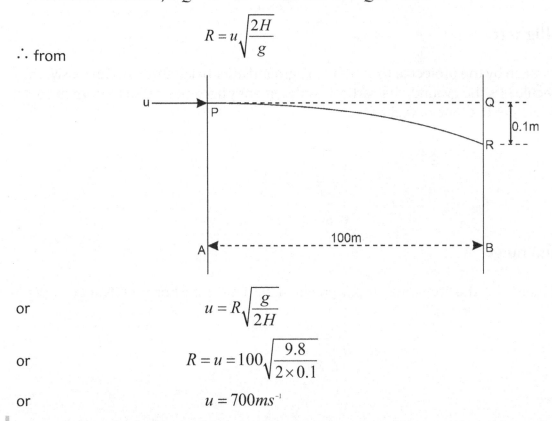

or
$$u = R\sqrt{\frac{g}{2H}}$$

or
$$R = u = 100\sqrt{\frac{9.8}{2 \times 0.1}}$$

or
$$u = 700 ms^{-1}$$

III. Projectile Fired from a Certain Height Above Ground with Upward Oblique Inclination with Horizontal

Suppose a projectile is thrown from a height H with its initial velocity $\vec{u}$ making an angle θ with the horizontal as shown below. Considering the point of throw as origin, horizontal direction as x-direction and vertically upward direction as y-direction, we have: $\vec{a} = -g\,\hat{j}$, that is, $a_y = -g$, $a_x = 0$, $u_x = u\cos\theta$ and $u_y = u\sin\theta$

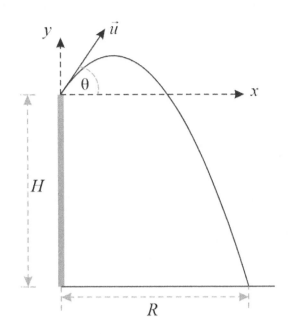

Motion in x-direction

I. $$v_x = u_x = u\cos\theta\cos^{-1}\theta$$

II. $$\Delta x = x = u\cos\theta\, t$$

Motion in y-direction

III. $$v_y = u\sin\theta - g\, t$$

IV. $$\Delta y = y = u\sin\theta\, t - \frac{1}{2}g\, t^2$$

1. Time of Flight (T)

It is the total time taken by the projectile to land on the ground after being thrown. Obviously, the moment the projectile hits the ground, the vertical displacement Δy becomes equal to $-H$. Therefore, from equation **IV.**, we get the time of flight by putting $\Delta y = -H$ and t = T:

$$g\, T^2 - 2u\sin\theta\, T - 2H = 0$$

We get,
$$T = \frac{u\sin\theta + \sqrt{u^2\sin^2\theta + 2gH}}{g}$$

2. Horizontal Range

From equation **II.**, put t = T, the horizontal displacement in this time is the horizontal range R. We get

$$R = u\cos\theta\, T$$

$$R = u\cos\theta\left(\frac{u\sin\theta + \sqrt{u^2\sin^2\theta + 2gH}}{g}\right)$$

Exercise 35

A ball is thrown up at an angle of 37^0 with the horizontal from a 50 m high tower with a speed of 25 m/s. Find its time of flight and its horizontal range.

Solution

Here we have, $v_x = u_x = u\cos\theta = 25 \times \frac{4}{5} ms^{-1} = 20 ms^{-1}$,

Therefore, $\Delta x = x = u(\cos\theta)t$ gives $\Delta x = (20 ms^{-1})t$ for any time.

Further, $u_y = u\sin\theta = 25 \times \frac{3}{5} ms^{-1} = 15 ms^{-1}$, therefore, $\Delta y = y = u\sin\theta t - \frac{1}{2}gt^2$ gives

$\Delta y = (15 ms^{-1})t - (5 ms^{-2})t^2$ for any time.

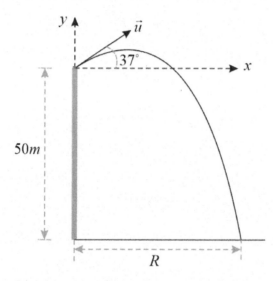

Time of Flight (T)

The moment the projectile hits the ground, the vertical displacement Δy becomes equal to $-50m$. Therefore, from above equation, we get the time of flight by putting $\Delta y = -50m$ and $\quad t = T$:

$$-50m = (15 ms^{-1})T - (5 ms^{-2})T^2$$

or $\qquad\qquad T^2 - 3T - 10 = 0 \qquad$ giving $\qquad\qquad T = 5s$

Horizontal Range

Putting $t = T = 5s$, in the equation $\Delta x = (20 ms^{-1})t$, the horizontal displacement in this time is the horizontal range R. We get

$$R = (20 ms^{-1}) \times 5s = 100m$$

IV. Projectile Fired from a Certain Height Above Ground with Downward Oblique Inclination with Horizontal

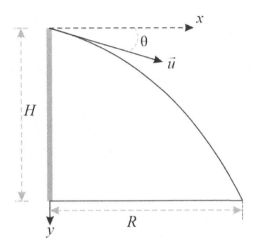

Suppose a projectile is thrown from a height H with its initial velocity $\vec{u}$ making an angle θ with the horizontal as shown below. Considering the point of throw as origin, horizontal direction as x-direction and vertically downward direction as y-direction, we have $\vec{a} = +g\,\hat{j}$, that is, $a_x = 0$, $a_y = +g$, $u_x = u\cos\theta$ and $u_y = u\sin\theta$

Motion in x-direction

I. $$v_x = u_x = u\cos\theta$$

II. $$\Delta x = x = u\cos\theta\, t$$

Motion in y-direction

III. $$v_y = u\sin\theta + g\,t$$

IV.   we get $$\Delta y = y = u\sin\theta\, t + \frac{1}{2}g\,t^2$$

1.   Time of Flight (T)

It is the total time taken by the projectile to land on the ground after being thrown. Obviously, the moment the projectile hits the ground, the vertical displacement y becomes equal to H. Therefore, from equation **IV.**, substituting $\Delta y = +H$ and t = T, we get the time of flight from:

$$g\,T^2 + 2u\sin\theta\,T - 2H = 0$$

we get, $$T = \frac{-u\sin\theta + \sqrt{u^2\sin^2\theta + 2gH}}{g}$$

2.   Horizontal Range

From equation **II.** substitute t = T, the horizontal displacement in this time is the horizontal range R. We get $$R = u\cos\theta\, T$$

$$R = u\cos\theta\left(\frac{-u\sin\theta + \sqrt{u^2\sin^2\theta + 2gH}}{g}\right)$$

Exercise 36

A ball is thrown down at an angle of 37^0 with the horizontal from a 50 m high tower with a speed of 25 m/s. Find its time of flight and its horizontal range.

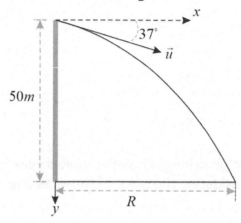

Solution

Here we have, $\qquad v_x = u_x = u\cos\theta = 25 \times \frac{4}{5} ms^{-1} = 20 ms^{-1}$

therefore, $\Delta x = x = u(\cos\theta)t$ gives $\Delta x = \left(20 ms^{-1}\right)t$ for any time

Further, $u_y = u\sin\theta = 25 \times \frac{3}{5} ms^{-1} = 15 ms^{-1}$, therefore, $\Delta y = y = u\sin\theta t + \frac{1}{2}g t^2$ gives

$\Delta y = \left(15 ms^{-1}\right)t + \left(5 ms^{-2}\right)t^2$ for any time.

Time of flight (t)

The moment the projectile hits the ground, the vertical displacement Δy becomes equal to $50m$. Therefore, from above equation, we get the time of flight by substitution $\Delta y = 50m$ and t = T:

$$50m = \left(15 ms^{-1}\right)T + \left(5 ms^{-2}\right)T^2$$

Or $\qquad\qquad\qquad\qquad T^2 + 3T - 10 = 0$

Giving $\qquad\qquad T = 2s$

Horizontal Range

Putting t = T = 5s, in the equation $\Delta x = \left(20 ms^{-1}\right)t$, the horizontal displacement in this time is the

horizontal range R. We get $R = \left(20 ms^{-1}\right) \times 2s = 40m$

V. *Projectile Thrown Over an Incline*

Consider an incline of inclination α. Suppose a projectile is thrown over it with its initial velocity $\vec{u}$ making an angle θ with the incline. To understand the motion of this projectile, it is better to take the x-axis along incline and y-axis perpendicular to the incline.

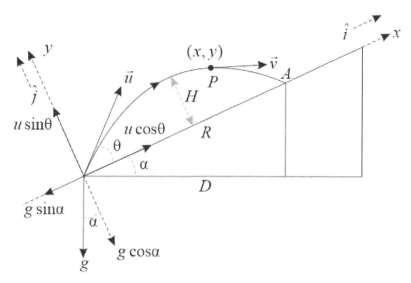

Clearly, the acceleration of the projectile is $\vec{a} = -g\sin\alpha\,\hat{i} - g\cos\alpha\,\hat{j}$ giving

$$a_x = -g\sin\alpha \text{ and } a_y = -g\cos\alpha$$

and initial velocity of the projectile $\vec{u} = u\cos\theta\,\hat{i} + g\sin\theta\,\hat{j}$ giving

$$u_x = u\cos\theta \text{ and } u_y = u\sin\theta$$

If the projectile reaches a point P (x, y) in time t, where its velocity is $\vec{v}$

Motion along x-direction

$$v_x = u_x + a_x t$$

I. $$v_x = u\cos\theta - (g\sin\alpha)t$$

and $$\Delta x = u_x t + \frac{1}{2}a_x t^2$$

II. gives $$x = u(\cos\theta)t - \frac{1}{2}(g\sin\alpha)t^2$$

Similarly,

Motion along y-direction

$$v_y = u_y + a_y t$$

III. gives $$v_y = u\sin\theta - g(\cos\alpha)t^2$$

and
$$\Delta y = u_y t + \frac{1}{2} a_y t^2$$

IV.   gives
$$y = u(\sin\theta)t - \frac{1}{2}(g\cos\alpha)t^2$$

1.   Time of Flight (T)

For time of flight substitute y = 0 in equation **IV.**,

$$0 = u(\sin\theta)t - \frac{1}{2}(g\cos\alpha)t^2$$

$$t\left[\frac{1}{2}(g\cos\alpha)t - u\sin\theta\right]^2 = 0$$

Giving
$$t = 0 \quad \text{and} \quad t = \frac{2u\sin\theta}{g\cos\alpha}$$

$\therefore$ Time of flight
$$T = \frac{2u\sin\theta}{g\cos\alpha} - 0$$

V.   i.e.,
$$T = \frac{2u\sin\theta}{g\cos\alpha} = \frac{2u_y}{|a_y|}$$

2.   Range Over Incline (R)

It is the displacement along x-direction in the total time of flight. In equation **II.** substitute $t = T = \dfrac{2u\sin\theta}{g\cos\alpha}$, we get x = R. Another method of finding range is using $R = \dfrac{D}{\cos\alpha}$ where D is the horizontal displacement of the projectile in the time equal to the time of flight.

thus
$$D = (u_{horizontal})T = \left[u\cos(\theta+\alpha)\right]\frac{2u\sin\theta}{g\cos\alpha}$$

$\therefore$
$$R = \frac{D}{\cos\alpha} = \frac{u\cos(\theta+\alpha)2u\sin\theta}{\cos\alpha(g\cos\alpha)}$$

VI.
$$R = \frac{2u^2\sin\theta.\cos(\alpha+\theta)}{g.\cos^2\alpha}$$

3.   Maximum Range

Using $2\sin A\cos B = \sin(A+B) + \sin(A-B)$, we can write,
$2\sin\theta\cos(\theta+\alpha) = \sin(2\theta+\alpha) - \sin(\alpha)$ and the range is written as

$$R = \frac{u^2}{g\cos^2\alpha}\{\sin(2\theta+\alpha) - \sin(\alpha)\}$$

for maximum value of R, $\sin(2\theta+\alpha)=1$ or $2\theta+\alpha=90^0$ or $\theta=45^0-\dfrac{\alpha}{2}$

Value of Maximum Range

$$R_{max}=\dfrac{u^2(1-\sin\alpha)}{g\cos^2\alpha}=\dfrac{u^2(1-\sin\alpha)}{g(1-\sin^2\alpha)}$$

VII.　or,
$$R_{max}=\dfrac{u^2}{g(1+\sin\alpha)}$$

4.　Maximum Height Over Incline (H)

It can be determined from the fact that at maximum height over incline $v_y=0$

Now using
$$v_y^2-u_y^2=2a_y\Delta y$$

putting　$v_y=0$, $u_y=u\sin\theta$, $a_y=-g\cos\alpha$, $\Delta y=H$,we get

$$0-u^2\sin^2\theta=-(2g\cos\alpha)H$$

VIII.　gives
$$H=\dfrac{u^2\sin^2\theta}{2g\cos\alpha}=\dfrac{u_y^2}{2|a_y|}$$

VI. Projectile Thrown Down an Incline

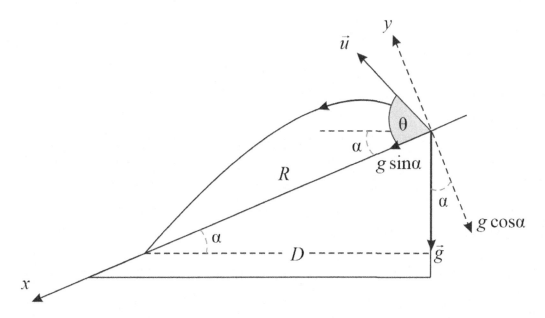

Consider an incline of inclination α. Suppose a projectile is thrown down it with its initial velocity $\vec{u}$ making an angle θ with the incline. To understand the motion of this projectile, it is better to take the x-axis along incline and y-axis perpendicular to the incline. Clearly, the acceleration of the projectile is

$$\vec{a}=+g\sin\alpha\,\hat{i}-g\cos\alpha\,\hat{j}$$

giving $\quad a_x = g\sin\alpha \qquad$ and $\qquad a_y = -g\cos\alpha$

and initial velocity of the projectile is $\vec{u} = u\cos\theta\,\hat{i} + g\sin\theta\,\hat{j}$

giving $\quad u_x = u\cos\theta \qquad$ and $\qquad u_y = u\sin\theta$

Motion along x-direction

$$\Delta x = u_x t + \frac{1}{2}a_x t^2 \quad \text{gives}$$

I.

$$x = (u\cos\theta)t + \frac{1}{2}(g\sin\alpha)t^2$$

Motion along y-direction

$$\Delta y = u_y t + \frac{1}{2}a_y t^2 \quad \text{gives}$$

II.

$$y = (u\sin\theta)t - \frac{1}{2}(g\cos\alpha)t^2$$

1. Time of Flight (T)

For time of flight substitute y = 0 in equation **II.**,

$$0 = (u\sin\theta)t - \frac{1}{2}(g\cos\alpha)t^2$$

$$\Rightarrow \qquad t\left[\frac{1}{2}(g\cos\alpha)t - u\sin\theta\right] = 0$$

giving $\qquad t = 0 \qquad$ and $\qquad t = \dfrac{2u\sin\theta}{g\cos\alpha}$

$\therefore \quad$ Time of flight $\qquad T = \dfrac{2u\sin\theta}{g\cos\alpha} - 0$

III. $\quad$ i.e., $\qquad T = \dfrac{2u\sin\theta}{g\cos\alpha} = \dfrac{2u_y}{|a_y|}$

2. Range Over Incline (R)

It is the displacement along x-direction in the total time of flight. In equation **I.**, substitute $t = T = \dfrac{2u\sin\theta}{g\cos\alpha}$, we get x = R. Another method of finding range is using $R = \dfrac{D}{\cos\alpha}$, where D is the horizontal displacement of the projectile in the time equal to the time of flight.

thus $\qquad D = \left(u_{horizontal}\right)T = \left[u\cos(\theta - \alpha)\right]\dfrac{2u\sin\theta}{g\cos\alpha}$

70

$\therefore$ $$R = \frac{D}{\cos\alpha} = \frac{u\cos(\theta-\alpha)2u\sin\theta}{\cos\alpha(g\cos\alpha)}$$

IV.   or $$R = \frac{2u^2\sin\theta.\cos(\theta-\alpha)}{g.\cos^2\alpha}$$

3.   Maximum Range

Using $2\sin A\cos B = \sin(A+B) + \sin(A-B)$, we can write

$2\sin\theta\cos(\theta-\alpha) = \sin(2\theta-\alpha) + \sin(\alpha)$

and the range is written as $R = \frac{u^2}{g\cos^2\alpha}\{\sin(2\theta-\alpha) + \sin(\alpha)\}$

for maximum value of R, $\sin(2\theta-\alpha) = 1$

$\Rightarrow$ $2\theta - \alpha = 90^0$ $\Rightarrow$ $\theta = 45^0 + \dfrac{\alpha}{2}$

Value of Maximum Range

$$R_{max} = \frac{u^2(1+\sin\alpha)}{g\cos^2\alpha} = \frac{u^2(1+\sin\alpha)}{g(1-\sin^2\alpha)}$$

$\Rightarrow$ $$R_{max} = \frac{u^2}{g(1-\sin\alpha)}$$

4.   Maximum Height Over Incline (H)

It can be determined from the fact that at maximum height over incline $v_y = 0$

Now using $$v_y^2 - u_y^2 = 2a_y\Delta y$$

Substituting $v_y = 0$, $u_y = u\sin\theta$, $a_y = -g\cos\alpha$, $\Delta y = H$,we get

$$0 - u^2\sin^2\theta = -(2g\cos\alpha)H$$

VI. $\Rightarrow$ $$H = \frac{u^2\sin^2\theta}{2g\cos\alpha} = \frac{u_y^2}{2a_y}$$

Exercise 37

Find the angle of inclination of an incline when it is found that maximum range down the incline is 3-times the maximum range over the incline.

Solution

$$R_{max}(up) = \frac{u^2}{g(1+\sin\alpha)}$$

$$R_{\max}(down) = \frac{u^2}{g(1-\sin\alpha)}$$

$$3\frac{u^2}{g(1+\sin\alpha)} = \frac{u^2}{g(1-\sin\alpha)}$$

$\Rightarrow \qquad 3(1-\sin\alpha) = (1+\sin\alpha)$

$\Rightarrow \qquad 3 - 3\sin\alpha = 1 + \sin\alpha$

$\Rightarrow \qquad 2 = 4\sin\alpha \quad$ or $\quad \alpha = 30°$

Exercise 38

A particle is projected horizontally with speed u from point A, which is 10m above the ground. If the particle hits the inclined plane perpendicularly at a point B, then find u. Take $g = 10 ms^{-2}$.

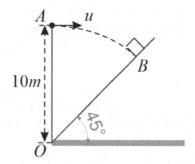

Solution

When the particle comes to point B in time t, its velocity v is equally inclined to the horizontal and the vertical. Therefore, $v_y = u$ but $v_y = gt \Rightarrow 10t = u$ or $t = \frac{u}{10}$. In this time the horizontal and the vertical displacements of the particle are $x = ut = \frac{u^2}{10}$ and $y = \frac{1}{2}gt^2 = 5\left(\frac{u^2}{100}\right) = \frac{u^2}{20}$.

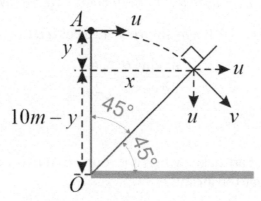

But as it is clear from the above figure that $x = 10 - y$

$$\frac{u^2}{10} = 10 - \frac{u^2}{20}$$

$\Rightarrow$ $$\frac{3u^2}{20} = 10$$

$\Rightarrow$ $$u = \sqrt{\frac{200}{3}} \ ms^{-1} = 10\sqrt{\frac{2}{3}} \ ms^{-1}$$

RELATIVE MOTION

Relative Motion of Two Objects

Relative Velocity of an object A with respect to another object B is defined as the time rate of change of separation of A from B. If $\vec{V}_A$ and $\vec{V}_B$ are the velocities of A and B with respect to a common observer O, then, the velocity of A with respect to B, written as $\vec{V}_{AB}$ is defined by

I.
$$\vec{v}_{AB} = \frac{d\vec{r}_{AB}}{dt}$$

Suppose at time t, the objects A and B have position vectors $\vec{r}_A$ and $\vec{r}_B$ with respect to the common observer O.

∴ The separation of A from B at time t is as follows $\vec{r}_{AB} = \vec{r}_A - \vec{r}_B \implies \vec{v}_{AB} = \dfrac{d\left(\vec{r}_A - \vec{r}_B\right)}{dt}$

II.
$$\implies \quad \vec{v}_{AB} = \frac{d\vec{r}_A}{dt} - \frac{d\vec{r}_B}{dt}$$

Since $\dfrac{d\vec{r}_A}{dt} = \vec{v}_A$ and $\dfrac{d\vec{r}_B}{dt} = \vec{v}_B$ are the velocities of A and B as seen by the common observer O,

∴   From equation **II.**,

III.
$$\vec{v}_{AB} = \vec{v}_A - \vec{v}_B$$

Differentiating equation **III.**, with respect to Time, we get the relative acceleration of A with respect to B as follows

IV.
$$\vec{a}_{AB} = \vec{a}_A - \vec{a}_B$$

I. When Two Objects are Moving Along Same Straight Line

We choose one direction to be positive and the opposite to be negative to simplify the vector algebra.

In this case when A and B both are moving along same direction, with $v_A = v_1$ and $v_B = v_2$, we get the following equation $v_{AB} = v_1 - v_2$

When A and B both are moving along opposite directions, with $v_A = -v_1$ and $v_B = v_2$, we get the following equation $v_{AB} = -v_1 - v_2 = -\left(v_1 + v_2\right)$

Exercise 39

A Police van is chasing a bike of goons with its maximum possible speed v. The bikers start their bike with constant acceleration a, when the police van is just x distance behind the bike. What should be the minimum value of v of the van so that the bikers are caught?

Solution

Let us study this problem by being a part of the bike, that is, relative to the bike. Let us take the direction of motion of the police van to be positive.

Initial relative velocity of the van with respect to bike: $u_{VB} = v - 0 = v$

Relative displacement of van with respect to bike: $S_{VB} = x$

Relative acceleration of van with respect to bike: $a_{VB} = 0 - a = -a$

The bikers will be caught only if the van comes ahead of the bikers within a relative displacement of x, that is, the velocity of the van is more than or equal to that of the bike at the time of catching.

$\therefore$ Final relative velocity of the bike with respect to van $v_{VB} \geq 0$

Now using $v^2 - u^2 = 2as$ for this relative motion, we get the following relations

$$v_{VB}^2 - v^2 = 2(-a)x$$

$\Rightarrow$
$$v_{VB}^2 = v^2 - 2ax$$

Since
$$v_{VB}^2 \geq 0$$

$\therefore$ $v^2 - 2ax \geq 0$ or $v \geq \sqrt{2ax}$

Thus, the minimum value of v is $\sqrt{2ax}$

Exercise 40

Two cars A and B cross a point P with velocities 10 m/s and 15 m/s. After that they move with different uniform accelerations and car A overtakes B with a speed of 25 m/s. What is the velocity of B at that instant?

Solution

Take a look at the following diagram

Taking the direction of motion of the cars to be positive, the accelerations of cars A and B to be a_A and a_B respectively, then initial velocity of A with respect to B and their relative acceleration are as follow

$$u_{AB} = (10 - 15)m/s = -5m/s$$

$$a_{AB} = a_A - a_B$$

When the car A overtakes car B, until that time relative displacement of A with respect to B is

$$x_{AB} = x_A - x_B = 0$$

Let the velocity of car B at this time be v_B, then the velocity of A with respect to B at this time is

$$v_{AB} = 25m/s - v_B$$

Therefore, using $v^2 - u^2 = 2as$ for this relative motion, we get

$$\left(25m/s - v_B\right)^2 - \left(-5m/s\right)^2 = 2\left(a_A - a_B\right)x_{AB}$$

$$\Rightarrow \qquad \left(25m/s - v_B\right)^2 - 25\left(m/s\right)^2 = 0$$

$$\Rightarrow \qquad \left(25m/s - v_B\right) = 5m/s \qquad \text{or} \qquad v_B = 20m/s$$

Exercise 41

A motor boat going downstream overcomes a float at a point A. 60 minutes later it turns and after some time passes the float at a distance 12 km from the point A. Assuming that the speed of boat in water (with respect to water) remains constant, find the velocity of the stream.

Solution

Let the speed of stream (water) be $v_w = u$ and that of the boat B in water be $v_{bw} = v$. If the velocity of boat with respect to ground is v_b, then from the value of relative velocity $v_{bw} = v_b - v_w$, we get $v_b = v_{bw} + v_w$, therefore,

(i) For downstream motion of the boat, $v_b = v + u$

(ii) For upstream motion of the boat, $-v_b = -v + u$ or $v_b = v - u$.

The float F goes on moving with the velocity of water $v_w = u$.

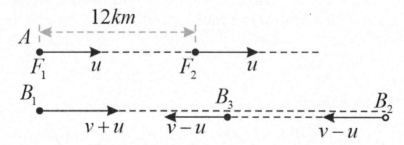

In one hour, the distance the boat goes downstream from B_1 to B_2, is given by

$$B_1 B_2 = \left(v + u\right) \times 1hr$$

After turning let's assume that it takes a time T to come across the float F again (that is, to come from B_2 to B_3)

$$\therefore \qquad B_2 B_3 = \left(v - u\right)T$$

As,
$$B_1 B_2 - B_2 B_3 = 12km$$

$$\therefore \qquad (v+u)\times 1hr-(v-u)T=12km$$

I. $\qquad\qquad \Rightarrow \qquad\qquad v(1hr-T)+u(1hr+T)=12km$

Since in this total time of $1hr+T$, the float itself has travelled a distance of 12km with a constant speed of u, therefore,

II. $$u(1hr+T)=12km$$

Comparing equations I. and II. $v(1hr-T)+u(1hr+T)=u(1hr+T)$

$$\Rightarrow \qquad v(1hr-T)=0 \qquad \Rightarrow \qquad T=1hr$$

Substituting T in equation II. gives us $u=6km/hr$

Exercise 42

Men are running in a line along a road with velocity 9km/h one behind the other at equal distances of 20m. Cyclists are also riding along the same line in the same direction at 18km/h one behind the other at equal distances of 30m. With what speed a lady on horse must travel along the road in opposite direction so that she meets each runner and a cyclist simultaneously.

Solution

Let the speed of the lady be v and meet a runner and a cyclist after a time period of T. It means, the displacement of the lady with respect to a runner in a time T is 20m and her displacement with respect to a cyclist in the same time is 30m. Therefore,

I. $$(v+9km/h)T=\frac{20}{1000}km \quad \text{and}$$

II. $$(v+18km/h)T=\frac{30}{1000}km$$

Dividing equation II. by equation I., we get,

$$\frac{(v+18km/h)}{(v+9km/h)}=\frac{30}{20}$$

$$\Rightarrow \qquad 2v+36km/h=3v+27km/h$$

$$\Rightarrow \qquad v=9km/h$$

II. Two Objects Moving in a Plane

In such cases we subtract the velocity vectors using vector algebra to get the desired result $\vec{v}_{AB}=\vec{v}_A-\vec{v}_B$. Following examples illustrate the same

A.   Some General Examples

Exercise 43

Wind is blowing due north-east with speed of 72 km/h and a ship is moving due north with a velocity of 51 km/h. Find in which direction the flag on the mast of ship will flutter. Given $72 \approx 51\sqrt{2}$.

Solution

The flag will flutter in the direction of the relative velocity of the wind with respect to the ship, which we will determine as follows

Let $\vec{v}_s$ and $\vec{v}_w$ represent the velocities of the ship and that of wind with respect to harbor, then the relative velocity of the wind with respect to the ship is $\vec{v}_{ws} = \vec{v}_w - \vec{v}_s$. Take a look at the following graphical representation of the velocity vectors involved, where angle $\alpha = 180^0 - \left(45^0 + \theta\right)$

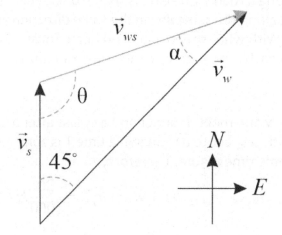

Using sine law for the triangle above,

$$\frac{\sin \alpha}{v_s} = \frac{\sin \theta}{v_w} \qquad \Rightarrow \qquad \frac{\sin\left\{180^0 - \left(45^0 + \theta\right)\right\}}{v_s} = \frac{\sin \theta}{v_w} \qquad \Rightarrow$$

$$\frac{\sin\left(45^0 + \theta\right)}{51} = \frac{\sin \theta}{72}$$

$$\Rightarrow \quad \frac{1}{\sqrt{2}}\frac{\left(\sin \theta + \cos \theta\right)}{51} = \frac{\sin \theta}{72} \quad \Rightarrow \quad \left(\sin \theta + \cos \theta\right) = \sin \theta$$

$$\Rightarrow \quad \cos \theta = 0 \quad \Rightarrow \quad \theta = 90^0$$

$\Rightarrow$ The flag on the mast of the moving ship flutters due east.

Exercise 44

Gun mounted at the rear part of a moving car is aimed in the backward direction at an angle of 60^0 with the horizontal. The muzzle velocity of the bullet fired from the gun is 80 m/s and it comes out vertical as seen from ground. Find the velocity of the car.

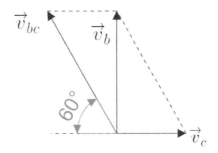

Solution

Let $\vec{v}_c$ and $\vec{v}_b$ represent the velocities of the car and that of bullet with respect to the ground, then the relative velocity of the bullet with respect to the car is $\vec{v}_{bc} = \vec{v}_b - \vec{v}_c$, therefore, $\vec{v}_b = \vec{v}_{bc} + \vec{v}_c$.

As it is given $\vec{v}_{bc}$ is inclined to horizontal at an angle of 60^0 and $\vec{v}_b$ is vertical, from the figure,

$$\frac{v_c}{v_{bc}} = \sin 30^0 \quad \Rightarrow \quad v_c = v_{bc} \sin 30^0 = 80 \times \frac{1}{2} m/s = 40 m/s$$

B.   *Rain-Umbrella Examples*

Exercise 45

Rain is falling vertically downward with respect to the ground with a speed of 16 km/h. A cyclist is riding due north with a speed of 12 km/h. In which direction should he hold his umbrella to protect himself from rain.

Solution

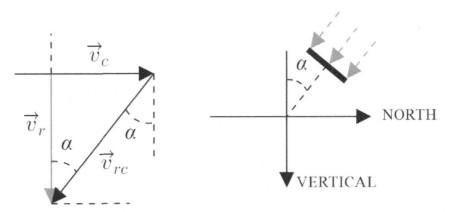

Let $\vec{v}_r$ and $\vec{v}_c$ represent the velocities of rain and cyclist with respect to the ground.

Given $\vec{v}_r$ = 16 km/h vertically downward

and $\vec{v}_c$ = 12 km/h due north

The cyclist should hold his umbrella against the relative velocity $\vec{v}_{rc}$ of rain with respect to himself. Therefore, we have to find the direction of $\vec{v}_{rc}$. Where $\vec{v}_{rc} = \vec{v}_r - \vec{v}_c$.

It is clear from the figure that $\vec{v}_{rc}$ makes an angle α with the vertical

$$\text{Tan}\,\alpha = \frac{V_c}{V_r} = \frac{12}{16} = \frac{3}{4}\text{ , therefore, } \alpha = 37°$$

Thus, the cyclist should hold his umbrella at an angle of 37° with the vertical due north.

Exercise 46

A cyclist riding due west with a speed of 12 km/h is holding his umbrella in vertical direction to protect himself from rain. Rain speed with respect to ground is 15 km/h. In which direction should a person standing on ground hold his umbrella? Also determine the rain speed with respect to the cyclist.

Solution

Given:

Velocity of cyclist with respect to the ground, $\vec{v}_c$ = 12 km/h due west

Speed of rain fall with respect to the ground, v_r = 15 km/h

Direction of relative velocity $\vec{v}_{rc}$ of rain with respect to the cyclist is vertically downward.

Direction of $\vec{v}_r$, with respect to ground is to be determined.

Now, $\vec{v}_{rc} = \vec{v}_r - \vec{v}_c$ $\Rightarrow$ $\vec{v}_r = \vec{v}_{rc} + \vec{v}_c$

It is determined as shown in the following figure

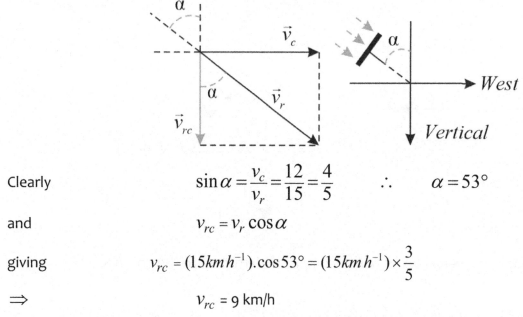

Clearly $\sin\alpha = \dfrac{v_c}{v_r} = \dfrac{12}{15} = \dfrac{4}{5}$ $\therefore$ $\alpha = 53°$

and $v_{rc} = v_r \cos\alpha$

giving $v_{rc} = (15\,km\,h^{-1}).\cos 53° = (15\,km\,h^{-1})\times\dfrac{3}{5}$

$\Rightarrow$ v_{rc} = 9 km/h

Thus, rain is falling 53° due west of vertical with respect to the ground and the man on ground will hold his umbrella 53° due east of vertical. Clearly rain speed with respect to the cyclist v_{rc} is 9 km/h.

Exercise 47

A cyclist is travelling with a speed of $7kmh^{-1}$ on a straight horizontal road. She is holding her umbrella vertically up. When she doubles her velocity, she has to hold her umbrella at an angle of 30° with the vertical. Find the velocity of rain with respect to the ground.

Solution

The vector algebra used is as follows $\qquad \vec{v}_{rc} = \vec{v}_r - \vec{v}_c \qquad \Rightarrow \qquad \vec{v}_r = \vec{v}_{rc} + \vec{v}_c$

Initially, velocity of cyclist with respect to the ground $\vec{v}_c = 7kmh^{-1}$ horizontally.

Direction of relative velocity of rain $\vec{v}_{rc}$ with respect to the cyclist is vertically downward.

Magnitude and direction of $\vec{v}_r$, with respect to the ground is to be determined.

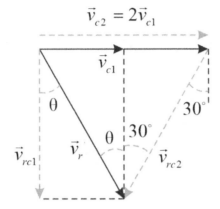

Let the direction of $\vec{v}_r$ makes angle θ with the vertical as drawn in the above diagram. $\vec{v}_r = \vec{v}_{rc1} + \vec{v}_{c1}$ is clearly drawn in the diagram above. When the velocity of the cyclist doubles, $\vec{v}_{rc2} = \vec{v}_r - \vec{v}_{c2}$ is drawn to make 30° with the vertical.

It is clear from the figure that the vertical line which is parallel to $\vec{v}_{rc1}$ is the right bisector of the base $2|\vec{v}_{c1}|$ of the triangle and hence bisect the vertical angle. Therefore, $\theta = 30^0$ and the triangle formed by vectors, $\vec{v}_r, 2\vec{v}_{c1} \ and \ \vec{v}_{rc2}$, is an equilateral triangle. Thus, $v_r = 2v_{c1} = 14kmh^{-1}$ and the direction of $\vec{v}_r$ makes the angle $\theta = 30^0$ with the vertical .

Exercise 48

A lady teacher is running down an incline of 37^0 with a speed of 5 m/s finds rain hitting her vertically. When she runs up the incline with the same speed, she finds rain getting down at an angle of $\tan^{-1}\dfrac{7}{8}$ with the horizontal. Find rain speed with respect to the ground.

Solution

(a) Lady teacher running down the incline   **(b) Lady teacher running up the incline**

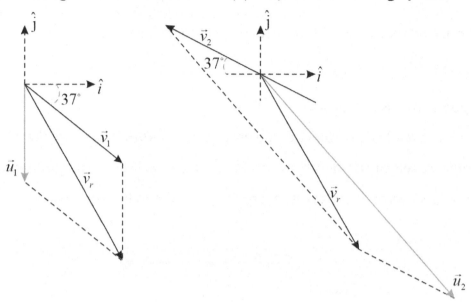

Let the velocity of rain with respect to the ground be $\vec{v}_r$, velocity of lady teacher in first case (when she is running down) be $\vec{v}_1$, then the velocity of rain with respect to her in this case will be $\vec{u}_1 = \vec{v}_r - \vec{v}_1$, giving $\vec{v}_r = \vec{v}_1 + \vec{u}_1$. Resolving along horizontal and vertical directions:

$\vec{v}_1 = \left(4\hat{i} - 3\hat{j}\right)m/s$ and $\vec{u}_1 = -u_1\,\hat{j}$,

I. $\therefore$ $\vec{v}_r = \left(4\hat{i} - 3\hat{j}\right)m/s - u_1\,\hat{j} = \left(4m/s\right)\hat{i} - \left(3m/s + u_1\right)\hat{j}$

Let the velocity of lady teacher in second case (when she is running up) be $\vec{v}_2$, then the velocity of rain with respect to her in this case will be $\vec{u}_2 = \vec{v}_r - \vec{v}_2$. Resolving along horizontal and vertical directions: $\vec{v}_2 = \left(-4\hat{i} + 3\hat{j}\right)m/s$.

Therefore, the vector $\vec{u}_2 = \vec{v}_r - \vec{v}_2$ is calculated as follows

$$\vec{u}_2 = \left\{\left(4m/s\right)\hat{i} - \left(3m/s + u_1\right)\hat{j}\right\} - \left(-4\hat{i} + 3\hat{j}\right)m/s$$

II. $\Rightarrow$ $\vec{u}_2 = \left(8m/s\right)\hat{i} - \left(6m/s + u_1\right)\hat{j}$

Clearly, $u_{2x} = 8m/s$ and $u_{2y} = 6m/s + u_1$. If $\vec{u}_2$ makes angle θ with the horizontal, then

$\tan\theta = \dfrac{u_{2y}}{u_{2x}} = \dfrac{6m/s + u_1}{8m/s}$. But it is given that $\tan\theta = \dfrac{7}{8}$, therefore, $\dfrac{6m/s + u_1}{8m/s} = \dfrac{7}{8}$ and we get,

$u_1 = 1m/s$. Therefore, equation I. gives $\vec{v}_r = \left(4m/s\right)\hat{i} - \left(4m/s\right)\hat{j}$ and we get $v_r = \left(4\sqrt{2}\right)m/s$.

C. Swimmer or a Boat Crossing a River

Let $\vec{v}_w$ be the velocity vector of river water (with respect to ground) and $\vec{v}_{mw}$ be velocity of swimmer (man) with respect to water and $\vec{v}_m$ is the velocity of man with respect to ground.

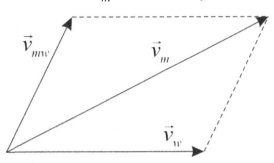

Since $\vec{v}_{mw} = \vec{v}_m - \vec{v}_w$

Therefore, $\vec{v}_m = \vec{v}_{mw} + \vec{v}_w$

The x-component of the velocity of the man with respect to ground (v_{m_x}) and the y-component of the velocity of the man with respect to ground (v_{m_y}) will be calculated as follows

$$v_{m_x} = v_{mw_x} + v_w \quad \text{and} \quad v_{m_y} = v_{mw_y}$$

As drawn in the figure below, these two relationships become

$$v_{m_x} = v_w - v_{mw}\sin\theta \text{ and} \quad v_{m_y} = v_{mw}\cos\theta$$

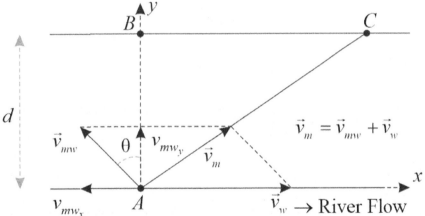

When the swimmer crosses the river from one bank to the other bank, he may go along AC as shown above. The distance BC is called the drift of the swimmer which is travelled by the swimmer with his velocity $v_{m_x} = v_w - v_{mw}\sin\theta$. The width of the river d is crossed by the swimmer with his velocity $v_{m_y} = v_{mw}\cos\theta$. Using just these two facts, using simple kinematics and calculus (if required), any problem related to river swimmer cases can be solved. Mostly there are two types of problems:

I. regarding the crossing time

II. regarding the value of drift.

These are discussed in detail as follows.

I. The Time of Crossing the River

As the component of the velocity of man along shore (v_{m_x}) is not responsible for its crossing the river. Only the component of velocity of man (v_{m_y}) along AB is responsible for its crossing along AB.

The time of crossing,

$$T = \frac{AB}{v_{mw} \cos\theta} = \frac{d}{v_{mw} \cos\theta}$$

Minimum crossing time

Time is minimum when $\cos\theta$ is maximum. The maximum value of $\cos\theta$ is 1 for $\theta = 0$.

That means the man should apply his strokes in water perpendicular to the shore

$\Rightarrow$
$$\vec{v}_{mw} \perp \vec{v}_w$$

Then
$$T_{\min} = \left(\frac{d}{v_{mw} \cos\theta}\right)_{\theta=0} = \frac{d}{v_{mw}}$$

$\Rightarrow$
$$T_{\min} = \frac{d}{v_{mw}}$$

In this case, the velocity of the man with respect to ground ($\vec{v}_m$) will be inclined to the shore at some acute angle as shown in the following figure.

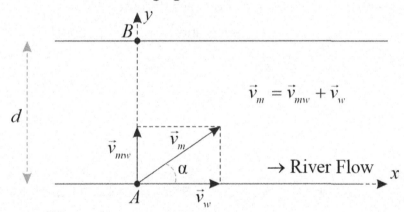

$$\vec{v}_m = \vec{v}_{mw} + \vec{v}_w$$

II.   The Drift

Suppose the man crosses the river in time T and the drifting of the man during this time when he reaches the opposite bank is BC = x

Then,
$$x = v_{m_x} T$$

Since,
$$v_{m_x} = v_w - v_{mw} \sin\theta$$

and,
$$T = \frac{d}{v_{mw} \cos\theta}$$

$\therefore$
$$x = (v_w - v_{mw} \sin\theta)\frac{d}{v_{mw} \cos\theta}$$

or
$$x = \left(\frac{v_w}{v_{mw}} \sec\theta - \tan\theta \right) d$$

Minimum drift

(i) No drift at all

For minimum drift, one may want **no** drift at all. For that the swimmer will reach the opposite bank at the point directly opposite to the stationary point. That is velocity of swimmer with respect to ground ($\vec{v}_m$) has to be perpendicular to the stream. In other words, the velocity of man parallel to shore must be zero

$$v_{m_x} = 0 \qquad \text{or} \qquad v_{m_y} = v_m$$

Which gives
$$0 = v_w - v_{mw} \sin\theta$$

or, by substituting,
$$(v_w - v_{mw} \sin\theta) \frac{d}{v_{mw} \cos\theta} = 0$$

we get
$$\sin\theta = \frac{v_w}{v_{mw}}$$

$\Rightarrow$
$$\theta = \sin^{-1}\left(\frac{v_w}{v_{mw}} \right)$$

Obviously, this can be possible only when $\sin\theta = \dfrac{v_w}{v_{mw}} < 1$, that is, when $v_w < v_{mw}$. In words, this is the case when swimmer is faster than river flow. **Thus, we observe that the drift can be zero only when the swimmer is faster than the river flow** and he applies his strokes in direction making an angle θ with the perpendicular to the stream which is given by

$$\sin\theta = \frac{v_w}{v_{mw}}$$

This case is demonstrated as follows:

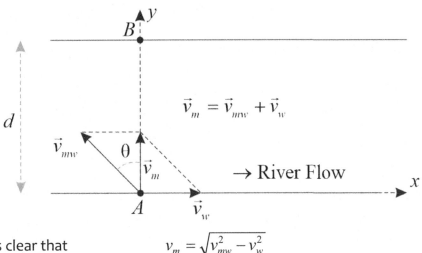

From the figure, is clear that
$$v_m = \sqrt{v_{mw}^2 - v_w^2}$$

The time of crossing

$$T = \frac{d}{v_{m_y}} = \frac{d}{v_m}$$

$\Rightarrow$

$$T = \frac{d}{v_{mw}\cos\theta} = \frac{d}{\sqrt{v_{mw}^2 - v_w^2}}$$

(ii) Minimum drift when River Flow is Faster than the Swimmer ($v_w > v_{mw}$)

As the drift cannot be zero when the river is faster, let us calculate what the minimum drift is to be

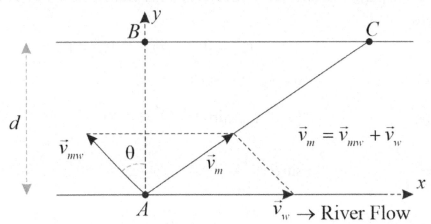

I.   As $x = (v_w - v_{mw}\sin\theta)\dfrac{d}{v_{mw}\cos\theta}$ $\Rightarrow$ $x = \left(\dfrac{v_w}{v_{mw}}\sec\theta - \tan\theta\right)d$

For x to be minimum, i.e., for minimum drift

$$\frac{dx}{d\theta} = \left(\frac{v_w}{v_{mw}}\sec\theta\tan\theta - \sec^2\theta\right)d = 0$$

$$\frac{v_w}{v_{mw}}\tan\theta = \sec\theta$$

$\Rightarrow$

$$\sin\theta = \frac{v_{mw}}{v_w} \quad \text{or} \quad \theta = \sin^{-1}\left(\frac{v_{mw}}{v_w}\right)$$

Substituting the value of θ in equation I., we obtain

$$x_{\min} = \left[\frac{\sqrt{v_w^2 - v_{mw}^2}}{v_{mw}}\right]d$$

Recap

I.   When swimmer is faster ($v_w < v_{mw}$), drift can be zero and for that the swimmer will have his velocity ($\vec{v}_m$) perpendicular to the river and direction of his strokes in water is given by

$$\sin\theta = \frac{v_w}{v_{mw}}$$

II.   When the river is faster ($v_w > v_{mw}$), drift can never be zero and for minimum drift, the swimmer will apply his strokes in water in direction given by $\sin\theta = \dfrac{v_{mw}}{v_w}$. In this case the velocity of swimmer with respect to ground ($\vec{v}_m$) will not be perpendicular to the stream and the minimum drift will be

$$x_{\min} = \left[\frac{\sqrt{v_w^2 - v_{mw}^2}}{v_{mw}}\right]d$$

III.   To reach directly opposite point on the other bank for a given $\vec{v}_{mw}$ & velocity $\vec{v}$ of walking along the shore in the minimum possible time

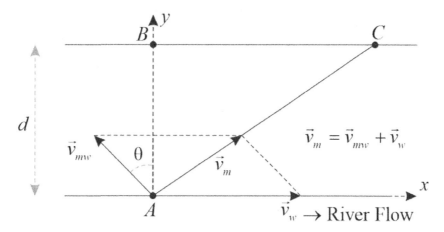

To attain the direct opposite point B in the minimum time. Let the man swim at an angle θ with the direction AB. The total time of journey t = (time taken from A to C) + (the time taken from C to B)

$$t = t_{AC} + t_{CB}$$

where $t_{AC} = \dfrac{AB}{v_{mw}\cos\theta}$ & $t_{CB} = \dfrac{BC}{v}$ where v = walking speed of the man from C to B.

I. $\Rightarrow \quad t = \dfrac{AB}{v_{mw}\cos\theta} + \dfrac{BC}{v}$

again $BC = v_{m_x}.t_{AC}$

II. $\Rightarrow \quad BC = \left(v_w - v_{mw}\sin\theta\right)\left(\dfrac{AB}{v_{mw}\cos\theta}\right)$

Using I. and II., we obtain,

$$t = \frac{AB}{v_{mw}\cos\theta} + \frac{(v_w - v_{mw}\sin\theta)AB}{v(v_{mw}\cos\theta)}$$

$$\Rightarrow \qquad t = AB\left(\frac{1}{v_{mw}\cos\theta} + \frac{\left(\dfrac{v_w}{v_{mw}} - \sin\theta\right)}{v\cos\theta}\right)$$

$$\Rightarrow \qquad t = AB\left[\frac{\sec\theta}{v_{mw}} + \frac{\dfrac{v_w}{v}\sec\theta}{v_{mw}} - \frac{\tan\theta}{v}\right]$$

$$\Rightarrow \qquad t = AB\left[\left(1 + \frac{v_w}{v}\right)\frac{\sec\theta}{v_{mw}} - \frac{\tan\theta}{v}\right]$$

Substituting $\dfrac{dt}{d\theta} = 0$ for minimum t we obtain

$$\frac{dt}{d\theta} = \frac{d}{d\theta}\left[\left(1 + \frac{v_w}{v}\right)\frac{\sec\theta}{v_{mw}} - \frac{\tan\theta}{v}\right] = 0$$

$$\Rightarrow \qquad \frac{dt}{d\theta} = \left[\frac{\sec\theta\tan\theta}{v_{mw}}\left(1 + \frac{v_w}{v}\right) - \frac{\sec^2\theta}{v}\right] = 0$$

$$\Rightarrow \quad \frac{\tan\theta}{v_{mw}}\left(1 + \frac{v_w}{v}\right) = \frac{\sec\theta}{v} \qquad \Rightarrow \quad \sin\theta = \left(\frac{v_{mw}}{v + v_w}\right) \qquad \Rightarrow \quad \theta = \sin^{-1}\left(\frac{v_{mw}}{v + v_w}\right)$$

This expression is obviously true when $v_{mw} < v + v_m$.

For Crossing with Minimum time

I. To reach the opposite bank for a given $\vec{v}_{mw}$ (and not to walk along the opposite bank to reach the point B), the swimmer will have to apply his strokes in water perpendicular to the stream.

In this case minimum crossing time is given by $t_{\min} = \dfrac{d}{v_{mw}}$ and $\sin\theta = 0$

II. To reach directly opposite point on the other bank for a given $\vec{v}_{mw}$ & velocity $\vec{v}$ of walking along the shore. In this case the strokes of man make some angle with the line perpendicular to the stream and

minimum crossing time is $t = AB\left[\left(1 + \dfrac{v_w}{v}\right)\dfrac{\sec\theta}{v_{mw}} - \dfrac{\tan\theta}{v}\right]$ and $\sin\theta = \left(\dfrac{v_{mw}}{v + v_w}\right)$. In all the previous

cases θ is the angle which the strokes of man in water ($\vec{v}_{mw}$) make with the line perpendicular to the shore.

Exercise 49

A man can walk on the shore at a speed v_1 = 6 km/h and swim in still water at a speed v_2 = 5 km/hr. If the speed of water is v_3 = 4 km/h, at what angle should he head in the river in order to reach the exact opposite of the shore in shortest time including his swimming & walking?

Solution

Directly using the previous result, we obtain the angle of swimming

$$\theta = \sin^{-1}\left(\frac{v_{mw}}{v + v_w}\right)$$

putting $v = v_1 = 6km/h$, $v_{mw} = v_2 = 5km/h$, $v_w = v_3 = 4km/h$ we obtain

$$\theta = \sin^{-1}\frac{1}{2} = 30°$$

The man should head at an angle of $\alpha = 90° + \theta = 120°$ with the direction of flow of water.

Exercise 50

The speed of a man in a pond is double that of the water in a river. The man starts swimming from a point A on the bank. What is the angle of swimming of the man so as to get directly to the opposite bank?

Solution

As $v_w < v_{mw}$, he can go across the river without any drift if he swims at an angle $90° + \theta$ with respect to water,

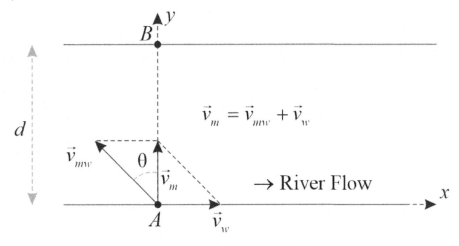

$$\sin\theta = \frac{v_w}{v_{mw}} \qquad \Rightarrow \qquad \theta = \sin^{-1}\frac{v_w}{v_{mw}}$$

We're given $v_{mw} = 2v_w \Rightarrow \dfrac{v_w}{v_{mw}} = \dfrac{1}{2} \qquad \Rightarrow \qquad \theta = \sin^{-1}\dfrac{1}{2} = 30°$

$\Rightarrow$ The angle of swimming $= 90° + \theta = 90° + 30° = 120°$ from the direction of flow of water.

Exercise 51

The speed of water is double that of swimmer (relative to water). What should be the direction of the swimmer so as to experience minimum displacement assuming $v_m = 5$ km/h?

Solution

Substituting the value $\dfrac{v_{mw}}{v_w} = \dfrac{1}{2}$ in the derived expression $\theta = \sin^{-1} \dfrac{v_{mw}}{v_w}$ we obtain

$$\theta = \sin^{-1} \frac{1}{2} = 30°$$

Exercise 52

A man crosses the river in shortest time at an angle $\alpha = 60°$ to the direction of flow of water as seen by a person sitting on shore. If the speed of water $v_w = 4$ km/h, find the speed of the man.

Solution

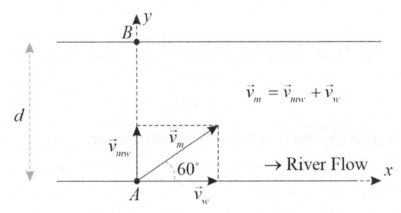

Referring to the theory, we know that for minimum time of crossing the man should head perpendicular to the shore $\qquad \vec{v}_{mw} \perp \vec{v}_w$

giving $\qquad v_{mw} = v_m \sin\theta \qquad$ and $\qquad v_w = v_m \cos\theta$

$\therefore \qquad \cos\theta = \dfrac{v_w}{v_m} \qquad\qquad \Rightarrow \qquad\qquad \cos 60° = \dfrac{4}{v_m}$

$\Rightarrow \qquad\qquad v_m = 8km / h$

Exercise 53

A man can swim in still water at 5 km/h. He has to cross a 1.0 km wide river flowing at a rate of 3 km/h. Determine

I.   The minimum time he will take to cross the river and drift.

II.   Value of minimum drift with the direction for achieving minimum drift and crossing time.

Solution

I.   For minimum crossing time $v_{m_y} = v_{mw} = 5 kmh^{-1}$

$$\therefore \qquad T_{min} = \frac{d}{v_{mw}} = \frac{1km}{5kmh^{-1}} = \frac{1}{5}h = 12\,min$$

During this time $v_{m_x} = v_w = 3kmh^{-1}$

$\therefore$ Drift equals $x = \left(3kmh^{-1}\right)\frac{1}{5}h = 0.6km$

II.   As $v_{mw} > v_w$, minimum drift will be zero drift and it will happen when the man applies his stokes at

$90° + \theta$ with the direction of water flow, where

$$\theta = \sin^{-1}\frac{v_w}{v_{mw}} = \sin^{-1}\frac{3}{5} = 37^0$$

In this case $v_{m_y} = v_{mw}\cos\theta = 5kmh^{-1}\frac{4}{5} = 4kmh^{-1}$

$\therefore$ Crossing time will be $T = \frac{d}{v_{m_y}} = \frac{1km}{4kmh^{-1}} = \frac{1}{4}h = 15\,min$

Exercise 54

A man can swim in still water at 3 km/h. He has to cross a 1.2km wide river flowing at a rate of 5 km/h. Determine

I.   The minimum time he will take to cross the river and drift.

II.   The value of minimum drift with the direction for achieving minimum drift and crossing time.

Solution

I.   For minimum crossing time $v_{m_y} = v_{mw} = 3kmh^{-1}$

$$\therefore \qquad T_{min} = \frac{d}{v_{mw}} = \frac{1.2km}{3kmh^{-1}} = \frac{1.2}{3}h = 24\,min$$

During this time $v_{m_x} = v_w = 5kmh^{-1}$

$\therefore$ Drift   equals $x = \left(5kmh^{-1}\right)0.4h = 2km$

II.   As $v_{mw} < v_w$, minimum drift cannot be zero. Therefore, for minimum drift the man will have to apply his stokes at $90° + \theta$ with the direction of water flow, where

$$\theta = \sin^{-1}\frac{v_{mw}}{v_w} = \sin^{-1}\frac{3}{5} = 37^0$$

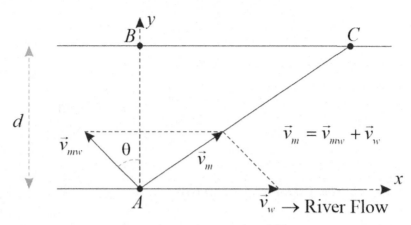

In this case

$$v_{m_y} = v_{mw} \cos\theta = 3kmh^{-1}\frac{4}{5} = \frac{12}{5}kmh^{-1}$$

∴ Crossing time will be

$$T = \frac{d}{v_{m_y}} = \frac{1.2km}{\frac{12}{5}kmh^{-1}} = 0.5h = 30\min$$

And,

$$v_{m_x} = v_w - v_{mw}\sin\theta = 5kmh^{-1} - \frac{3}{5}\left(3kmh^{-1}\right) = \frac{16}{5}kmh^{-1}$$

∴ Minimum Drift equals

$$x_{\min} = \frac{16}{5}kmh^{-1}\left(0.5h\right) = 1.6km$$

D.   Motion of an Airplane Relative to Wind

In this type of relative motion usually the velocity of wind and the relative velocity of plane with respect to the wind is given and the velocity of plane with respect to ground is to be analyzed, the vector algebra to be used is

$$\vec{v}_{PW} = \vec{v}_P - \vec{v}_W \qquad \text{or} \qquad \vec{v}_P = \vec{v}_{PW} + \vec{v}_W$$

Exercise 55

An airplane has to go due east from an air-base A to another air-base B. The wind is blowing at a velocity of 70km/h, $16°$ due east of north. The speed of plane with respect to the air is 240km/h. Find the direction along which the pilot must point the plane and also determine velocity of plane with respect to ground, and time taken if the destination is 500km away. Given, $\sin 74° \cong 24/25$ and $\sin 16° \cong 7/25$.

Solution

$\vec{v}_P = \vec{v}_{PW} + \vec{v}_W$ has to point due east, $v_{PW} = 240kmh^{-1}$ and $v_W = 70kmh^{-1}$ therefore from the following diagram

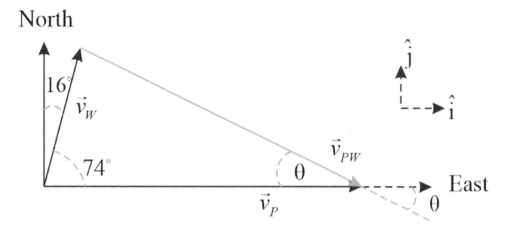

using sine law of triangle, it is clear that

$$\frac{v_{PW}}{\sin 73^{o}} = \frac{v_W}{\sin \theta}, \text{ which gives, } \frac{240}{\frac{24}{25}} = \frac{70}{\sin \theta},$$

that is, $\qquad \sin \theta = \frac{7}{25} \quad \Rightarrow \theta \cong 16^o$ and so, $v_p = 250km/h$

The pilot will steer the plane $\theta \cong 16^o$ due south of east, the speed of plane with respect to ground will be 250 km/h and the plane will take 2 hours to reach from A to B.

Exercise 56

An Airplane has to go from an air-base A to another air-base B which is 500km away and east of north from it. The wind is blowing at a velocity of 20m/s, due north. The speed of plane with respect to air is 150m/s. Find the direction along which the pilot must point the plane and also determine velocity of plane with respect to the ground, and time taken to reach B.

Solution

Here $\vec{v}_P = \vec{v}_{PW} + \vec{v}_W$ has to point 30° east of north,

$v_{PW} = 150m/s \qquad$ and $\qquad v_W = 20m/s$

Therefore, from the following diagram:

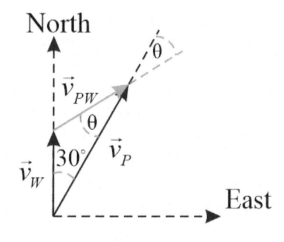

using sine law of triangle, it is clear that

$$\frac{v_{PW}}{\sin 30^o} = \frac{v_W}{\sin \theta} = \frac{v_P}{\sin(\theta + 30^o)}, \text{ which gives,}$$

that is, $\sin \theta = \dfrac{1}{15}$ or $\theta = \sin^{-1}\dfrac{1}{15}$, and so, $v_P = 300ms^{-1}\sin(\theta + 30^o) = 167.3ms^{-1}$

$$t = \frac{500000m}{167.3ms^{-1}} = 2988.6s = 49.8\,min$$

The pilot will steer the plane $\theta = \sin^{-1}\dfrac{1}{15}$ due east of line AB, the speed of plane with respect to

the ground will be $167.3ms^{-1}$ and the plane will take $49.8\,min$ to reach from A to B.

E.   *Relativity of Two Objects Approaching Each Other*

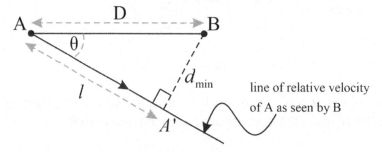

Consider the motion of two objects, say A and B, along two different paths in a plane. Knowing their initial separation and their initial velocities, we have to find

I.   The distance of their closest approach.

II.   The time taken by them to be closest to each other.

If their initial velocities are $\vec{v}_A$ and $\vec{v}_B$ (with respect to a common observer) and their accelerations are same so that their relative velocity $\vec{v}_{AB} = \vec{v}_A - \vec{v}_B$ does not change with time, then the solution of

the problem is very simple and following steps are recommended:

1.   Draw a figure showing initial positions of A and B with the initial separation, say D, between them.

2.   Considering one of them, say B, as stationary show the motion of the other, that is, of A along the line of the relative velocity $\vec{v}_{AB}$. In fact, B would see A moving with $\vec{v}_{AB}$. This is shown as follows:

3.   A will be closest to B when $\vec{v}_{AB}$ has no component towards B, that is, when the line of $\vec{v}_{AB}$ becomes perpendicular to the line joining A and B. In the above figure, it happens when A reaches to A'. When A reaches A', the line joining A and B, that is, $A'B$ becomes perpendicular to the line of $\vec{v}_{AB}$. Clearly the distance $A'B = d_{min}$ is the distance of closest approach of A and B. To find it, we drop perpendicular from B on the line of $\vec{v}_{AB}$, the length of this perpendicular (d_{min}), is the distance of closest approach of A and B. From the above figure $d_{min} = D\sin\theta$

where θ is the angle between the line of $\vec{v}_{AB}$ and the initial line joining A and B.

4.   Before the two objects be closest, A will have to travel a distance $AA' = l = D\cos\theta$ with the relative speed v_{AB}, therefore, the time taken by them to come closest is $t = \dfrac{D\cos\theta}{v_{AB}}$

Exercise 57

Two ships A and B are moving with same speed 20 km/h. At an instant ship B is seen 20km south of ship A and at this instant A is seen moving due south whereas B is seen moving due east (both with respect to harbor). Find the minimum distance between the two ships and the time after which they will be nearest to each other.

Solution

Take a look at the following figure showing B at rest and A moving relative to B with relative velocity $\vec{v}_{AB} = \left(20\sqrt{2}\ kmh^{-1}\right)\ south-west$ with initial separation between them equal to D = 20 km.

Clearly, $d_{min} = D\sin\theta = \left(20km\right)\sin 45° = 10\sqrt{2}\ km$

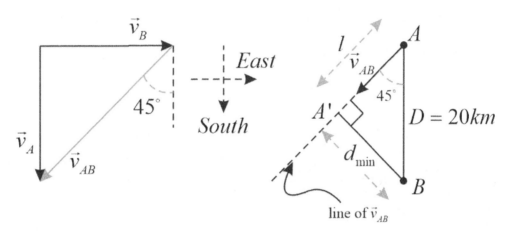

Further, $l = D\cos 45° = \left(20km\right)\cos 45° = 10\sqrt{2}\ km$ and $v_{AB} = \left(20\sqrt{2}\ kmh^{-1}\right)$

$\therefore$ $t = \dfrac{D\cos\theta}{v_{AB}} = \dfrac{10\sqrt{2}\ km}{20\sqrt{2}\ kmh^{-1}} = \dfrac{1}{2}h$

ALTERNATE METHOD

We can also determine d_{min} and t using calculus method. In the following figure the positions of ship A and ship B after time t are shown. Both have travelled the same distance $r = vt = \left(20km/h\right)t$ in time t, with A moved due south and B moved due east.

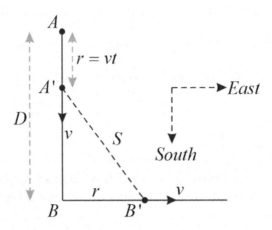

At this time, the distance between A and B is given by

$$S^2 = r^2 + (D-r)^2 = 2r^2 + D^2 - 2Dr$$

When S will be minimum S^2 will also be minimum and at that time $\dfrac{d(S^2)}{dr} = 0$, so by differentiating

S^2 with respect to r, we get $\dfrac{d(S^2)}{dr} = 4r - 2D$, substituting $\dfrac{d(S^2)}{dr} = 0$, we obtain $r(=vt) = \dfrac{D}{2}$.

This shows that the ships will be closest to each other when both would have travelled a distance

$$r(=vt) = \dfrac{D}{2}$$

This gives, $\quad d^2{}_{min} = S^2{}_{min} = \dfrac{D^2}{4} + \dfrac{D^2}{4} \quad\quad \Rightarrow \quad\quad d_{min} = \dfrac{D}{\sqrt{2}} = 10\sqrt{2}\ km$

and from $r(=vt) = \dfrac{D}{2}$, we get $t = \dfrac{20km}{2(20km/h)} = \dfrac{1}{2}h$.

Exercise 58

Two particles, A and B are moving in a plane with constant relative velocity of magnitude v. Initially when the distance between them is D, the component of their relative velocity along the line joining them is v_1 and perpendicular to that line is v_2. Find the minimum distance between the them and the time after which they will be nearest to each other.

Solution

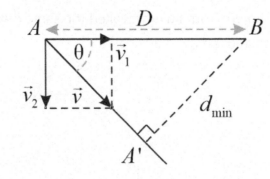

From the following figure it is clear that $\cos\theta = \dfrac{v_1}{v}$ and $\sin\theta = \dfrac{v_2}{v}$.

Therefore, $d_{min} = D\sin\theta = \dfrac{Dv_2}{v}$ and $t = \dfrac{D\cos\theta}{v_{AB}} = \dfrac{Dv_1}{v^2}$

Exercise 59

Two projectiles A and B are thrown from ground as shown in the figure. Find along which direction projectile A appears flying to projectile B. Also find the minimum distance between them and the time after which they will be nearest to each other ($\sin 23° \approx 5/13$ & $\cos 23° \approx 12/13$)

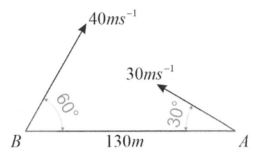

Solution

Velocities of projectiles, A and B at any time are $\vec{v}_A = \vec{u}_A + \vec{g}t$ and $\vec{v}_B = \vec{u}_B + \vec{g}t$, therefore, $\vec{v}_{AB} = \vec{u}_A - \vec{u}_B =$ constant. From the following figure it is clear that the magnitude of $\vec{v}_{AB}$ is $50ms^{-1}$ and it is every time $23°$ below the horizontal line passing through B .Thus to the projectile B it will appear that the projectile A is flying along the straight line $23°$ below the horizontal line passing through it.

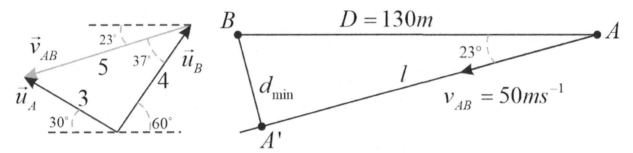

Clearly, $d_{min} = D\sin\theta = (130\,m)\sin 23° = 50m$ and $t = \dfrac{D\cos\theta}{v_{AB}} = \dfrac{120m}{50ms^{-1}} = 2.4s$

Exercise 60

Two projectiles A and B are thrown from ground as shown in figure-1 given below.

I.   If $\theta = 37°$, find u_A so that the two projectiles collide.

II.   Suppose u_A to be such that the projectile A appears flying to the projectile B moving below it at an angle of $8°$ with horizontal, find u_A. Also find the minimum distance between them and the time after which they will be nearest to each other.

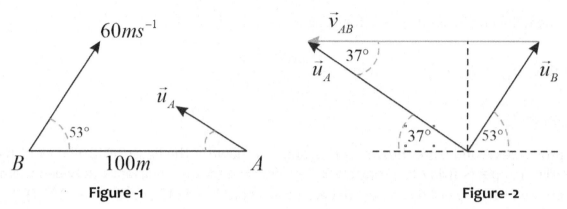

Figure -1   **Figure -2**

Solution

I.   If $\theta = 37^o$ (figure-2 above), then for the projectiles to collide, the line of the relative velocity $\vec{v}_{AB}$ must be passing through B, that is, it must be parallel to the initial line AB or the vertical components of both $\vec{u}_A$ and $\vec{u}_B$ must be same. Both the logics suggest $\dfrac{u_A}{u_B} = \cot 37^o = \dfrac{4}{3}$, that is, $u_A = 80m/s$.

II.   In this case, it is clear from the following figure that $u_A = u_B = 60m/s$

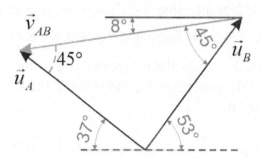

And $v_{AB} = 60\sqrt{2}ms^{-1}$, therefore, from the following figure,

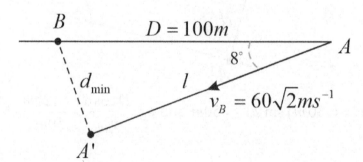

$$d_{min} = D\sin\theta = (100m)\sin 8^o \qquad \text{and} \qquad t = \dfrac{D\cos\theta}{v_{AB}} = \dfrac{100m\cos 8^o}{60\sqrt{2}ms^{-1}} = \dfrac{5\cos 8^o}{3\sqrt{2}}s$$

Exercise 61

Two particles A and B are projected simultaneously from two points O' and O such that d is the horizontal distance and h is the vertical distance between them as shown in the figure. These are projected at same inclination α with the horizontal with same speed v. Find an expression for time at which their separation becomes minimum.

Solution

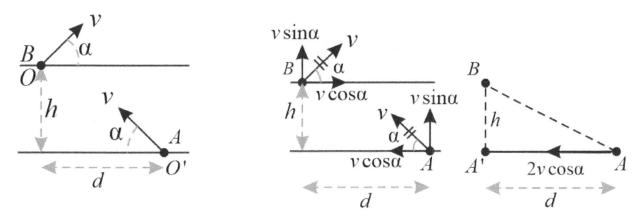

As it is clear from the figure, the two projectiles have same vertical velocity, the vertical separation between them is not going to change, it will remain same equal to h. Their relative velocity is horizontal, the projectile A appears to B, moving horizontally towards it with relative velocity $2v\cos\alpha$ at a height h below it.

Obviously, A will be closest to B when it reaches A' just vertically below it .In this time it has covered a horizontal distance d with a velocity $2v\cos\alpha$, therefore, the time taken as follows is the time when the projectiles are closest to each other.

$$t = \frac{d}{2v\cos\alpha}$$

KINEMATICS OF CIRCULAR MOTION

Angular Position of a Particle

At some instant of time, the angle θ made by the position vector, $\vec{r}$, of the particle with a reference line (say x-axis) is called its angular position .

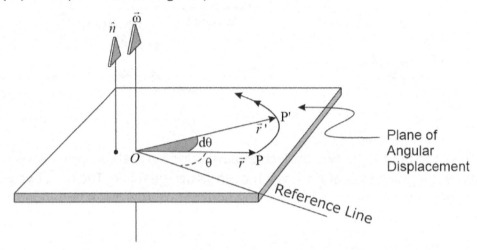

Angular Displacement as a Vector Quantity

When the angular position of the particle changes then the angle swept by the position vector of the particle is called its angular displacement.

Infinitely-small angular displacements are considered as vectors. The direction of an infinitely small angular displacement $d\vec{\theta}$ (as shown above) is taken perpendicular to the plane of angular motion according to the right hand screw rule.

Usually finite angular displacements are not considered as vectors as they do not satisfy the rules of vector addition. In case the finite angular displacements are all in same plane they too are considered as vectors.

Angular Velocity Vector ($\vec{\omega}$)

Angular velocity of a particle at an instant is defined as the rate of change of its angular position $\vec{\omega} = \dfrac{\overrightarrow{d\theta}}{dt}$. It is measured in $rad.s^{-1}$ and its direction is that of the angular displacement $d\vec{\theta}$, that is, perpendicular to the plane of angular motion according to the right hand screw rule.

Angular Acceleration Vector ($\vec{\alpha}$)

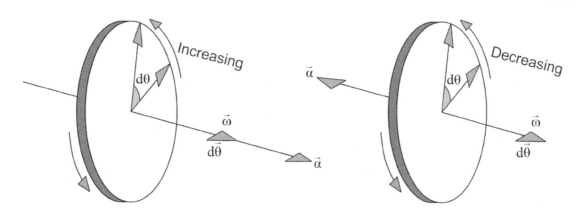

Angular acceleration of a particle at an instant is defined as the rate of change of its angular velocity $\vec{\alpha} = \dfrac{\overrightarrow{d\omega}}{dt}$. It is measured in $rad.s^{-2}$ and its direction is that in which angular velocity changes, that is, in the direction of $\vec{\omega}$ if it is increasing and opposite to $\vec{\omega}$ if it is decreasing.

Kinematical Relations Between Angular Variables When Plane of Motion Does Not Change

From $\qquad \alpha = \dfrac{d\omega}{dt} \qquad$ we get $\qquad \Delta\omega = \int\limits_0^t \alpha\, dt$

giving $\qquad \omega = \omega_0 + \int\limits_0^t \alpha\, dt$

and from $\qquad \omega = \dfrac{d\theta}{dt} \qquad$ we get $\qquad \Delta\theta = \int\limits_0^t \omega\, dt$

giving $\qquad \Delta\theta = \omega_0 t + \int\limits_0^t \left(\int\limits_0^t \alpha\, dt \right) dt$

If $\alpha = $ constant then, above equations give

$$\omega = \omega_0 + \alpha t \,,\ \Delta\theta = \omega_0 t + \frac{1}{2}\alpha t^2 \text{ and } \omega^2 = \omega^2_{\ 0} + 2\alpha\,\Delta\theta$$

Three Mutually Perpendicular Unit Vectors Important for Studying Angular Motion Along a Circle

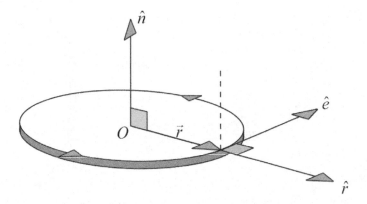

Three mutually perpendicular unit vectors $\hat{n}$, $\hat{r}$ and $\hat{e}$ are such that at a point on the circle, $\hat{n}$ is perpendicular to the plane of the circle, $\hat{r}$ is radially outward along the radius of the circle and $\hat{e}$ is tangential to the circle.

It can be clearly seen from the figure that, $\hat{n} \times \hat{r} = \hat{e}$, $\hat{r} \times \hat{e} = \hat{n}$ and $\hat{e} \times \hat{n} = \hat{r}$.

As it can be seen in the above figure that $\hat{n}$ remains fixed whereas $\hat{e}$ and $\hat{r}$ rotate when the particle moves in circle.

Motion of a particle in a circle

Consider a particle moving on a circle of radius R. Let the center of the circle to be the origin of coordinates and at a time t the particle is at position P with position vector $\vec{r} = r\hat{r}$. The angular position of the particle is measured from x-axis and let it is θ at this time.

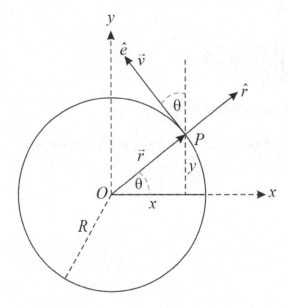

The velocity of the particle at this time is $\vec{v}$ and its angular velocity is $\vec{\omega}$. Where $\vec{v} = \dfrac{d\vec{r}}{dt}$ and

$\vec{\omega} = \dfrac{d\vec{\theta}}{dt}$ It must be noted that the angular speed $\omega = \left|\dfrac{d\vec{\theta}}{dt}\right| = \dfrac{d\theta}{dt}$ as the direction of angular

displacements does not change (plane of motion does not change). The speed $v = \left|\dfrac{d\vec{r}}{dt}\right| \neq \dfrac{dr}{dt}$

because the direction of $\vec{r}$ is continuously changing. Let us find the relation between v, ω and the acceleration of the particle at any instant.

It is clear from the figure that the x and y coordinates of the particle are

$$x = r\cos\theta \qquad \text{and} \qquad y = r\sin\theta$$

∴   The position vector of the particle at any time t is

I.
$$\vec{r} = x\hat{i} + y\hat{j} = r\left(\cos\theta\,\hat{i} + \sin\theta\,\hat{j}\right)$$

∴   The radial unit vector equals

II.
$$\hat{r} = \dfrac{\vec{r}}{r} = \cos\theta\,\hat{i} + \sin\theta\,\hat{j}$$

And, the tangential unit vector $\hat{e}$ which is perpendicular to $\hat{r}$ is given by

III.
$$\hat{e} = -\sin\theta\,\hat{i} + \cos\theta\,\hat{j}$$

Differentiating equation II. and equation III. with respect to time, we get

$$\dfrac{d\hat{r}}{dt} = \left(-\sin\theta\,\hat{i} + \cos\theta\,\hat{j}\right)\dfrac{d\theta}{dt}$$

that is,

IV.
$$\dfrac{d\hat{r}}{dt} = \omega\hat{e}$$

And
$$\dfrac{d\hat{e}}{dt} = \omega\left(-\sin\theta\,\hat{i} - \cos\theta\,\hat{j}\right)$$

That is,

V.
$$\dfrac{d\hat{e}}{dt} = -\omega\hat{r}$$

As we know
$$\vec{v} = \dfrac{d\vec{r}}{dt} = \dfrac{d\left(r\hat{r}\right)}{dt}$$

In a circular motion $r = R =$ radius of circle $=$ constant,

∴
$$\vec{v} = r\dfrac{d\hat{r}}{dt} \qquad \text{substituting} \qquad \dfrac{d\hat{r}}{dt} = \omega\hat{e}$$

we get,

VI.
$$\vec{v} = r\omega\hat{e} = R\omega\hat{e}$$

That is, the instantaneous velocity is tangential to the circle every time and the speed is related to angular speed by the relation $v = r\omega = R\omega$.

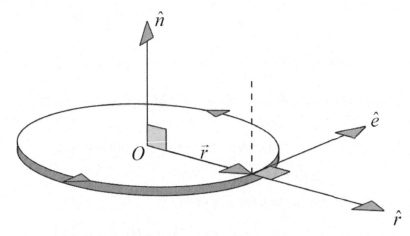

$\hat{n} \times \hat{r} = \hat{e}$, $\hat{r} \times \hat{e} = \hat{n}$ and $\hat{e} \times \hat{n} = \hat{r}$

Using the above diagram and unit vectors $\hat{n}$, $\hat{r}$ and $\hat{e}$ we can write $\vec{v} = r\omega\hat{e} = R\omega\hat{e}$ as

$$\vec{v} = \omega r(\hat{n} \times \hat{r}) = (\omega\hat{n}) \times (r\hat{r}) \qquad \text{or}$$

VII.
$$\vec{v} = \vec{\omega} \times \vec{r}$$

Further the acceleration is $\quad \vec{a} = \dfrac{d\vec{v}}{dt}$

$\therefore \quad$ from equation **VI.**
$$\vec{a} = \frac{d(r\omega\hat{e})}{dt} = r\frac{d(\omega\hat{e})}{dt}$$

or
$$\vec{a} = r\hat{e}\frac{d\omega}{dt} + r\omega\frac{d\hat{e}}{dt}$$

substituting $\dfrac{d\hat{e}}{dt} = -\omega\hat{r}$ in the above expression for acceleration, we get

VIII.
$$\vec{a} = \left(r\frac{d\omega}{dt}\right)\hat{e} + r\omega^2(-\hat{r})$$

In the above expression, we see that the acceleration has the following two components

(i) The component $\left(r\dfrac{d\omega}{dt}\right)\hat{e}$ is tangential to the path, we call it tangential acceleration $\vec{a}_{\text{tan}}$

and

(ii) The component $r\omega^2(-\hat{r})$ is directed radially inwards, towards the center, we call it radial or centripetal acceleration $\vec{a}_c$ (or $\vec{a}_r$).

In this way the acceleration of the particle is written as follows

IX.
$$\vec{a}=\vec{a}_{\tan}+\vec{a}_c$$

Tangential Acceleration

(i) The tangential acceleration comes out to be

X.
$$\vec{a}_{\tan}=\left(r\frac{d\omega}{dt}\right)\hat{e}=\alpha\,r\,\hat{e}=\hat{e}\frac{d(r\omega)}{dt}=\hat{e}\frac{dv}{dt}$$

Clearly, the magnitude of tangential acceleration $a_{\tan}=\alpha\,r=\dfrac{dv}{dt}$ gives the rate change of speed.

It is directed along the velocity vector when speed is increasing $\left(\dfrac{dv}{dt}\ is\ positive\right)$ and it is

directed opposite to the velocity vector when speed is decreasing $\left(\dfrac{dv}{dt}\ is\ negative\right)$. Using $\hat{n},\ \hat{r}$

and $\hat{e}$ we can write it as follows

XI.
$$\vec{a}_{\tan}=\alpha\,r\,\hat{e}=\alpha\,\hat{n}\times r\,\hat{r}=\vec{\alpha}\times\vec{r}$$

Centripetal or Radial Acceleration

(ii) The centripetal or radial acceleration comes out to be

XII.
$$\vec{a}_c=\omega^2\,r\left(-\hat{r}\right)=\frac{v^2}{r}\left(-\hat{r}\right)$$

Radial acceleration is related to the continuous change in the direction of velocity vector. Using $\hat{n}$, $\hat{r}$ and $\hat{e}$ we can write it as follows

XIII.
$$\vec{a}_c=\left(\omega\hat{n}\right)\times\left(r\,\omega\hat{e}\right)=\vec{\omega}\times\vec{v}$$

Uniform Circular Motion

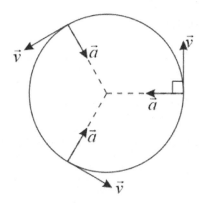

In this case $\quad \alpha = 0$ or $\quad \dfrac{dv}{dt} = 0$, i.e., $\quad \vec{a}_{\tan} = \vec{0}$, therefore, $\vec{a} = \vec{a}_c \quad$ everywhere towards

center and $\quad$ in magnitude, $\qquad\qquad a = a_c = \omega^2 r = \dfrac{v^2}{r}$

Non-Uniform Circular Motion

A.   Speeding Up Motion

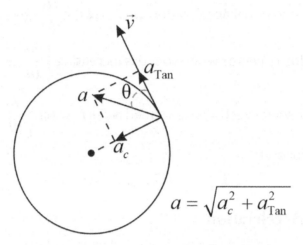

$$a = \sqrt{a_c^2 + a_{\text{Tan}}^2}$$

In this case $\qquad\qquad \alpha > 0$ or $\dfrac{dv}{dt} > 0$, i.e., $\vec{a}_{\tan}$ is along $\vec{v}$

Therefore, $\vec{a} = \vec{a}_{\tan} + \vec{a}_c$, everywhere makes acute angle $\theta = \tan^{-1}\left(\dfrac{a_c}{a_{\tan}}\right)$ with $\vec{v}$

In magnitude, $\qquad a = \sqrt{a_{\tan}^2 + a_c^2} = \sqrt{\alpha^2 r^2 + \omega^4 r^2} = \sqrt{\left(\dfrac{dv}{dt}\right)^2 + \omega^4 r^2}$

Exercise 62

A particle starts from rest to move along a circle of radius 2m. It's speed increases at a constant rate of $2ms^{-2}$. Find its acceleration at time t = 2s.

Solution

It is given $\qquad\qquad a_{\tan} = \dfrac{dv}{dt} = 2ms^{-2} \qquad \Rightarrow \qquad dv = \left(2ms^{-2}\right)dt$

After integration, we get $v = \left(2ms^{-2}\right)t \quad \Rightarrow \qquad v = 4ms^{-1} \quad$ (at t = 2s)

$\therefore \qquad\qquad\qquad\qquad a_c = \dfrac{v^2}{r} = \dfrac{\left(4ms^{-1}\right)^2}{2m} = 8ms^{-2}$

$$\therefore a = \sqrt{a_{\tan}^2 + a_c^2} = \left(\sqrt{4+64}\right)ms^{-2} = \left(\sqrt{68}\right)ms^{-2} \quad \text{and} \quad \theta = \tan^{-1}\left(\frac{a_c}{a_{\tan}}\right) = \tan^{-1}4$$

B.   Slowing-Down Circular Motion

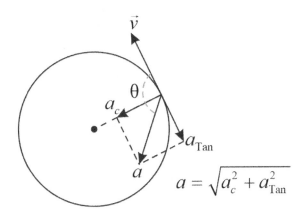

$$a = \sqrt{a_c^2 + a_{\tan}^2}$$

In this case $\alpha < 0$ or $\dfrac{dv}{dt} < 0$ i.e., $\vec{a}_{\tan}$ is opposite to $\vec{v}$

Therefore, $\vec{a} = \vec{a}_{\tan} + \vec{a}_c$, everywhere makes obtuse angle θ with $\vec{v}$

in magnitude, $a = \sqrt{a_{\tan}^2 + a_c^2} = \sqrt{\alpha^2 r^2 + \omega^4 r^2} = \sqrt{\left(\dfrac{dv}{dt}\right)^2 + \omega^4 r^2}$

Exercise 63

A particle is moving in a circle of radius R with speed changing with time as $v = bt$, where b is a constant. Find the acceleration of the particle when it has covered n times the circle.

Solution

Because $v = bt$, therefore, $a_{\tan} = \dfrac{dv}{dt} = b$

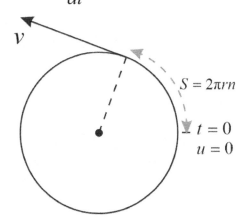

Since $a_{\tan} = \alpha R$ therefore $\alpha = \dfrac{d\omega}{dt} = \dfrac{b}{R}$

Now $\qquad \dfrac{d\omega}{dt} = \dfrac{b}{R} \qquad \Rightarrow \qquad \dfrac{d\omega}{dt}d\theta = \dfrac{b}{R}d\theta \qquad \Rightarrow \qquad \omega\, d\omega = \dfrac{b}{R}d\theta$

integration yields $\qquad \dfrac{\omega^2}{2} = \dfrac{b}{R}2\pi n$

$\Rightarrow \qquad a_c = \omega^2 R = 4\pi b n$

Further $\qquad a = \sqrt{a_{\tan}^2 + a_c^2}$

$\Rightarrow \qquad a = \sqrt{b^2 + \left(4\pi b n\right)^2}$

GENERAL CURVILINEAR MOTION OF A PARTICLE IN A PLANE

Consider a particle moving in a plane in a general curve. At some instant of time its position vector is $\vec{r}$ and it makes an angle θ with the reference line. In an infinitely small time dt, let its position vector become $\vec{r}' = \vec{r} + \overline{dr}$ and angular position becomes $\theta + d\theta$. Here it must be carefully noted that $|\overline{dr}| \neq dr$. Care must be taken in understanding the difference between $|\overline{dr}|$ and dr, it must be kept in mind that dr is the radial increment in the size of r, that is, dr is that which comes in $r' = r + dr$.

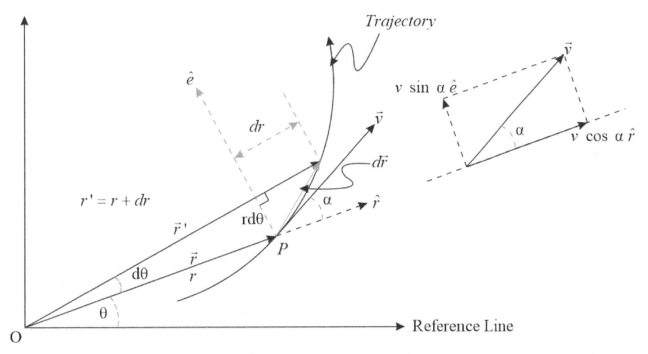

Clearly, from the figure
$$\frac{dr}{rd\theta} = \tan(90^0 - \alpha) \quad \Rightarrow \quad dr = (r\cot\alpha)d\theta \qquad \text{I.}$$

$$\Rightarrow \quad \frac{dr}{r} = (\cot\alpha)d\theta$$

To get a calculative study of such a general motion, consider a situation in which the velocity vector ($\vec{v}$) remains inclined to the position vector ($\vec{r}$) at a constant angle. Let us first find the expressions for the trajectory of the particle in terms of r and θ (polar coordinates).

If (r_0, θ_0) are the coordinates of the particle at zero time, then by integrating the equation I. from zero time to time t, that is, from (r_0, θ_0) to (r, θ), we get

$$\int_{r_0}^{r} \frac{dr}{r} = \int_{\theta_0}^{\theta} (\cot\alpha)d\theta$$

$$\Rightarrow \quad \ln\frac{r}{r_0} = (\theta - \theta_0)\cot\alpha$$

II.
$$\Rightarrow \quad r = r_0 e^{(\theta-\theta_0)\cot\alpha} = r_0 \exp\{(\theta-\theta_0)\cot\alpha\}$$

Three Special Cases

1. If $\alpha = 90^0$, we get $r = r_0 =$ constant, and the particle moves in a circle

2. If $\alpha < 90^0$, $\cot\alpha$ is positive, we find that r goes on increasing with time as θ is increasing one (sense of motion is not changing) and the particle moves in an outward spiral

3. If $\alpha > 90^0$, $\cot\alpha$ is negative, we find r goes on decreasing with time and the particle moves in an inward spiral.

Further, as we know $\vec{v} = \dfrac{d\vec{r}}{dt} = \dfrac{d(r\hat{r})}{dt}$

$\therefore$
$$\vec{v} = \hat{r}\frac{dr}{dt} + r\frac{d\hat{r}}{dt}$$

substituting $\quad \dfrac{dr}{dt} = v_r \quad$ and $\quad \dfrac{d\hat{r}}{dt} = \omega\hat{e}$

gives

III.
$$\vec{v} = \hat{r}v_r + r\omega\hat{e}$$

where $\quad v_r = \dfrac{dr}{dt} = v\cos\alpha =$ radial component of velocity

and $\qquad\qquad v_\theta = r\omega = v\sin\alpha =$ the component of velocity revolving with θ

It must be noted that $v_\theta \neq v_{\tan}$ rather $\vec{v}_{\tan}$ is the velocity $\vec{v}$ itself.

1. If $\alpha = 90^0$, $v_r = \dfrac{dr}{dt} = v\cos\alpha = 0$ and in this case $v_\theta = r\omega = v\sin\alpha = v = v_{\tan}$. The motion is along a circle.

2. If $\alpha < 90^0$, $\cot\alpha$ is positive, showing that the particle moves in an outward spiral

3. If $\alpha > 90^0$, $\cot\alpha$ is negative, showing that the particle moves in an inward spiral

Let us calculate the acceleration of the particle as follows

$$\vec{a} = \frac{d\vec{v}}{dt} = \frac{d}{dt}\left(\hat{r}\frac{dr}{dt} + \hat{e}\omega r\right)$$

or
$$\vec{a} = \left(\hat{r}\frac{d^2r}{dt^2} + \frac{dr}{dt}\frac{d\hat{r}}{dt}\right) + \left(\frac{d\hat{e}}{dt}\omega r + \hat{e}r\frac{d\omega}{dt} + \hat{e}\omega\frac{dr}{dt}\right)$$

substituting $\dfrac{d\hat{r}}{dt} = \omega\hat{e}$, $\dfrac{d\hat{e}}{dt} = -\omega\hat{r}$ and $\dfrac{d\omega}{dt} = \alpha$ in the equation above gives

$$\vec{a} = \left(\hat{r} \frac{d^2 r}{dt^2} + \hat{e}\omega \frac{dr}{dt} \right) + \left(-\hat{r}\omega^2 r + \hat{e}\alpha r + \hat{e}\omega \frac{dr}{dt} \right)$$

IV. $\qquad \Rightarrow \qquad \vec{a} = \left(\frac{d^2 r}{dt^2} - \omega^2 r \right)\hat{r} + \left(\alpha r + 2\omega \frac{dr}{dt} \right)\hat{e}$

It is clear from the above that when the radial distance is changing (spiral motion), the radial component of acceleration has an additional term $\hat{r} \dfrac{d^2 r}{dt^2}$ along with the usual centripetal term $-\hat{r}\omega^2 r$ and the component of acceleration revolving with θ has an additional term $2\omega \dfrac{dr}{dt}\hat{e}$ along with the usual term $\alpha r \hat{e}$. Clearly, if the motion is along a circular arc $\dfrac{dr}{dt} = 0$, $\dfrac{d^2 r}{dt^2} = 0$ and the acceleration will reduce to $\vec{a} = \alpha r \hat{e} - \hat{r}\omega^2 r$.

Tangential and Normal Acceleration and Radius of Curvature

In case of general curvilinear motion, the better way of analyzing the acceleration is resolving it into the tangential and normal acceleration. $\dfrac{dv}{dt}$ is given by the tangential component of acceleration which is in the direction of or opposite to $\vec{v}$. The normal acceleration, which is also the component of acceleration perpendicular to $\vec{v}$ plays the same role as that is played by centripetal acceleration in circular motion, that is, for changing the direction of the velocity.

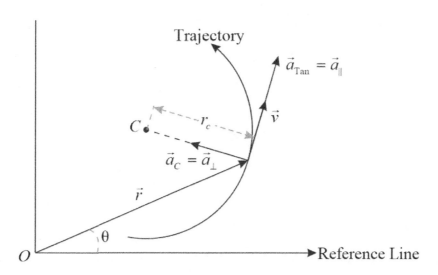

Furthermore, the normal acceleration can be used to find the radius of curvature of the path at any point of the trajectory. Radius of curvature at a given point on the path is the radius of the complete circle drawn from a differential arc taken at that point. If a_c or $a_\perp$ is the normal acceleration at a point on the path, v is the speed of the particle at that point, the radius of curvature r_c of the path at that point can be obtained from the relation $a_c = \dfrac{v^2}{r_c}$.

Exercise 64

Twelve particles lie on the 12 corners of a regular polygon of side a. Now they start moving towards each other with constant speed v in such a way that one always heads towards the next. Find

I.   time after which they meet

II.   displacement and distance travelled by each particle before they meet

III.   equation of trajectory of each particle (in polar coordinates).

Solution

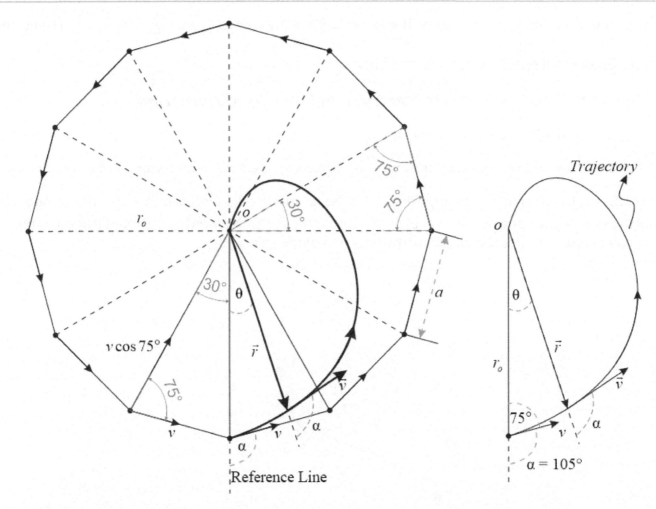

It can be seen from the following figure that if the center to corner distance is taken r_0, then

$$a = 2r_0 \sin 15^o, \text{ which gives} \qquad r_0 = \frac{a}{2\sin 15^o}$$

It is clear that the particles will meet at the center of the polygon. So, the displacement of each particle will be r_0 before they meet. As $v\cos 75^o$ is the component of the velocity of each particle towards the center every time, therefore, the time taken by each to meet (to reach the center) is given by

$$t = \frac{r_0}{v\cos 75^o} = \frac{a}{2v\cos 75^o \sin 15^o} = \frac{a}{2v\sin^2 15^o}$$

$$\Rightarrow \qquad t = \frac{a}{v\left(1 - \cos 30^o\right)} = \frac{2a}{v\left(2 - \sqrt{3}\right)}$$

If S is the distance travelled by each particle before all the particles meet, then S = v t, and we obtain the following relation

$$S = v\left\{\frac{2a}{v\left(2 - \sqrt{3}\right)}\right\} = \frac{2a}{\left(2 - \sqrt{3}\right)}$$

In general, if there are n such particles on the corners of a n sided regular polygon then

$$r_0 = \frac{a}{2\sin\dfrac{\pi}{n}}, \qquad t = \frac{a}{v\left(1 - \cos\dfrac{2\pi}{n}\right)} \qquad \text{and} \qquad S = \frac{a}{\left(1 - \cos\dfrac{2\pi}{n}\right)}$$

Every time each particle moves along the direction making an angle of $\alpha = 105^o$ with its position vector $\vec{r}$ drawn from the center of the polygon. If this position vector makes angle θ at any time with the reference line which is taken along the initial position vector $\vec{r}_0$, this angle goes on increasing from $\theta_0 = 0^o$, the equation of the trajectory comes out to be

$$r = r_0\, e^{\left(\theta - \theta_0\right)\cot\alpha} = r_0 \exp\left\{\left(\theta - \theta_0\right)\cot\alpha\right\}$$

substituting $r_0 = \dfrac{a}{2\sin 15^o}$, $\theta_0 = 0^o$ and $\cot\alpha = \cot 105^o = -\tan 15^o$, the equation above becomes

$$r = \left(\frac{a}{2\sin 15^o}\right) e^{\left(-\tan 15^o\right)\theta} = \left(\frac{a}{2\sin 15^o}\right)\exp\left\{\left(-\tan 15^o\right)\theta\right\}$$

This equation is one of an inward spiral.

Exercise 65

A projectile is thrown at an angle θ with the horizontal with speed u. Find its rate of change of speed, normal acceleration and radius of curvature of the path at

I. The initial point,   II. at the top of the trajectory.

Solution

At point A, the component of $\vec{a} = -\hat{j}g$ along the initial velocity $\vec{u}$ is given by

$$a_{tan} = \frac{dv}{dt} = -g\sin\theta = \text{the rate of change of speed}$$

and

$$a_{normal} = g\sin\theta$$

113

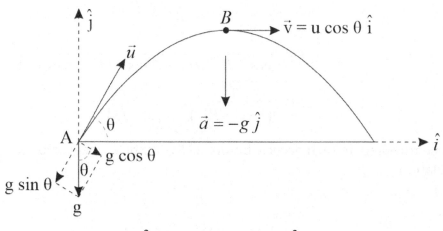

since $\qquad a_{normal} = a_c = \dfrac{v^2}{r_c}$, therefore, $r_c = \dfrac{u^2}{g\cos\theta}$

At the topmost point B $a_{tan} = 0$ and $a_{normal} = g$,

therefore, $\qquad r_c = \dfrac{v^2}{a_{normal}}$

or $\qquad r_c = \dfrac{u^2 \cos^2\theta}{g}$

Exercise 66

A dog is heading towards cat with constant speed v and the cat is running with constant velocity $\vec{u}$, where v > u. Initially the cat is l distance away from the dog and it is running perpendicular to the line joining them. Find the time T after which the cat is caught by the dog.

Solution

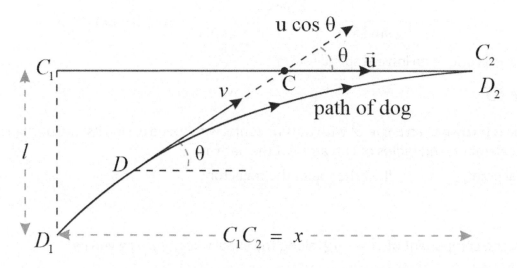

Let at time t, DC = S. As $v > u\cos\theta$, the velocity of approach of dog towards cat is $v - u\cos\theta$.

Therefore, $\qquad \dfrac{-dS}{dt} = v - u\cos\theta$

Giving $$-dS = (v - u\cos\theta)dt$$

Integrating $$-\int_l^0 dS = \int_0^T (v - u\cos\theta)dt$$

I. $$\Rightarrow \quad l = vT - u\int_0^T \cos\theta \, dt$$

The component of dog's velocity along the line C_1C_2 which is $v\cos\theta$, is variable but it is this variable velocity with which the dog covers the distance $C_1C_2 = x$ in time T to catch the cat.

Therefore, $$\frac{dx}{dt} = v\cos\theta \quad \Rightarrow \quad dx = v\cos\theta \, dt$$

II. $$\Rightarrow \quad x = v\int_0^T \cos\theta \, dt$$

But the cat covers this $C_1C_2 = x$ in time T with constant speed u, therefore,

III. $$x = uT$$

From equations, II. and III., we obtain the following relations

IV. $$v\int_0^T \cos\theta \, dt = uT$$

V. $$\Rightarrow \quad \int_0^T \cos\theta \, dt = \frac{uT}{v}$$

From equations I. and V., we obtain the following relations

$$l = vT - u\left(\frac{uT}{v}\right)$$

$$\Rightarrow \quad l = \frac{v^2T - u^2T}{v}$$

$$\Rightarrow \quad T = \frac{lv}{(v^2 - u^2)}$$

Made in the USA
Las Vegas, NV
14 November 2023

80832037R00070